ANNIHILATION ZONES

credits

ANNIHILATION ZONES

Stephen Barber

ISBN 1-84068-065-2

Published by Creation Books 2002

www.creationbooks.com

Copyright © Stephen Barber 2002

All world rights reserved

photo credits: Roger Hunt Library; Jack Hunter Collection

contents

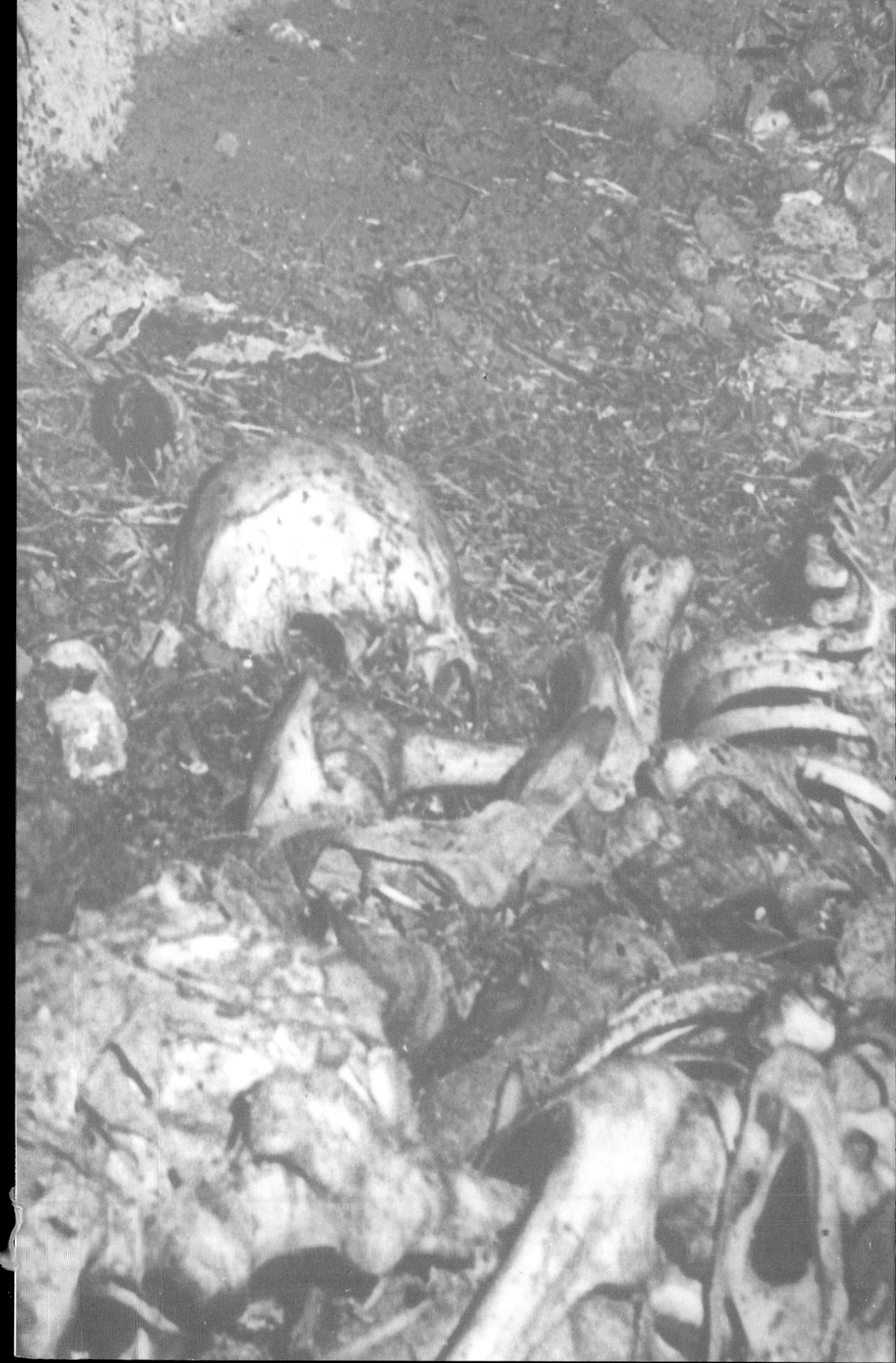

Introduction
The Traces Of Slaughter

Give me crack and anal sex

Take the only tree that's left

and stuff it up the hole

in your culture

Give me back the Berlin Wall

Give me Stalin and Saint Paul

I've seen the future, brother:

it is murder.

–Leonard Cohen, *The Future* (1992)

East Asia's twentieth century was marked out by an incandescent series of projects of slaughter that continue to illuminate the present and future, both of that region, and also of Europe and the United States. In East Asia, the twentieth century became an experimental testing-ground for all-out cruelty, atrocity, sexual servitude, degradation, cannibalism, violation, and human mass-elimination. The exacting of violence and subjugation on entire populations passed far beyond all corporeal extremities, engendering a new, terminal vision of the human body itself. East Asia is vitally mapped by a network of annihilation zones – the lethal scars and permanent aberrations that became impacted into the forms of the region over the twentieth century, and whose presence also determines East Asia's future direction. That vast work of butchery was resolutely carried-through by a series of tyrants whose obsessional projects are distinguished by an utterly uncompromised will to obliterate both their own populations and often those of other regions too: the Japanese Emperor Hirohito, together with his generals and the director of his 'Unit 731' bacteriological mass-extermination research centre, Shiro Ishii; the Soviet dictator Josef Stalin, who – in terms of sheer millions of victims – rose to become the twentieth century's premium instigator of gratuitous carnage; and Pol Pot, the Paris-educated tyrant whose ambitious project to transform Cambodia into a decimated wilderness of enslaved or brutally-massacred inhabitants accords him the status of East Asia's ultimate obliterator.

This book begins in Japan, with an account of Hirohito's plan to subjugate the entirety of East Asia to his divinely-endowed will, through a colonial holocaust that extended from Manchuria in the north, down to New Guinea in the south. The Unit 731 death-experimentation centre, with its plague-attacks on cities and its fourteen-year regime of live-dissections and eviscerations, formed the originating core of an ever-expanding empire of slaughter which finally overstretched itself, resulting in the self-cannibalism of abandoned armies and finally backfiring into a summary retribution that saw Japan itself turned into a firestormed wasteland of destroyed cities and vaporized populations, while the USA seized control of Unit 731's precious data for future application in the twentieth-century's subsequent conflicts. To the north of Japan, on the extreme edge of East Asia, the Soviet dictator Josef Stalin created the immense death-city of Magadan, where fourteen million of his own subjects would be relentlessly clubbed, frozen, mass-raped and arbitrarily gunned-down in a vast sub-zero landscape of ice, incinerated human ashes and butchered bodies, whose sequel is still to be unleashed upon the world. Stalin's determined acts exerted a crucial stimulus for many of the massacre-crazed tyrants of the final decades of the twentieth century. Finally, this book travels to the southern edge of East Asia, to end with the first-ever in-depth exploration of the preoccupations that drove the Stalin-inspired Cambodian dictator, Pol Pot, to turn the inhabitants of a small country into the raw materials for a colossal project of subjugation, sustained torture and terminal slaughter.

This account of East Asia's annihilation zones is drawn from many years of research, interviews and travels, from the consultation of primary sources, and from the discovery of numerous new materials (often on the neglected sexual dynamics that were integral to the strategies of cruelty and decimation pursued by East Asia's outstanding figures of despotic control). The seminal and spectacular power of atrocity, in the contemporary world, is often at odds with the power of the media and with their reprehensible dilution of the memory of atrocity: the contemporary media, together with the lacklustre cliques of academia, have specialized in banalizing and casting into oblivion many of the key events and compulsions that will certainly come to determine the course of the next century in East Asia, as well as in Europe and the USA. Combating that banalization of atrocity is a central aim of this book, and will necessarily make it a visceral and sensorially extreme experience for its reader. But such experiences are essential and salutary for all those who need to understand the contemporary world, together with the layers of rampant slaughter which underpin it. This book explores the obsessions that made the perpetrators of mass-obliteration act with their uncompromised sense of mission and will, in order to radically overhaul the status of the human body and to corrosively probe the nature of the human species itself. The result of those projects was the often-capricious culling of many millions of East Asia's inhabitants, whose fate is vitally resuscitated by this book. The ghost traces of East Asia's great projects of slaughter are brought to life again here.

Part One
Japan: Lust For Death

HIROHITO: THE DESIRE FOR ALL-OUT BUTCHERY

During the years from 1931 to 1945, Japan determinedly undertook the twentieth-century's supreme mission of slaughter, combining the bacteriological obliteration of entire cities with the cannibalism and crucifixion of prisoners of war, the mass-bayoneting and sexual violation of urban populations, and the arbitrary overhaul and eradication of human life. Almost all of those who devised and carried through Japan's vast project of lethal subjugation, across East Asia, escaped retribution and were rewarded after the conflict with high social status, as was the case with the staff of Unit 731, the immense human-experimentation complex whose scientists were devoted to planning the wholesale decimation of Japan's enemies via the unleashing of plague-attacks, and undertook their prestigious, imperially-sanctioned research by dissecting alive and eviscerating many thousands of civilian test-subjects. In the end, Japan's great aim – to realize a regime of cataclysmic carnage and sexual submission that would extend right across East Asia and beyond – became overstretched to breaking point and rapidly disintegrated into self-immolation, leading to the summary incineration and A-bombing of a large part of Japan's urban population, and infusing the country with a profound scar of capricious butchery and sensory overkill which is still deeply etched into contemporary Japan, with its own regime of schoolchildren's massacres, its lethal cultist attacks, and its cities of devastating neural excess.

Japan, in the years when the gratuitous pursuit of extreme atrocity became elevated to a universal system of operation, was the imperial domain of

Hirohito, whose lineage stretched back unbroken to the gods of thunder, bad blood and sexual aberrance who had created Japan in an era when myth had abruptly become reality. Hirohito was a sickly, myopic child whose father, a slavering cretin, had been the imperial figurehead of the Taisho era, whose regime of relatively benevolent government and cultural experimentation came to an end with the death of Hirohito's father on 25 December 1926. Hirohito then became the third in a new series of god-Emperors whose supremacy had been restored after the overturning in 1868 of centuries of draconian rule over Japan by generations of military warlords who had sidelined the imperial family. The young Hirohito had been the first Japanese Emperor to visit Europe, hoping to establish himself within the great community of emperors and monarchs who ruled most of the world via their colonial possessions; but his condescending counterparts in the British royal family had cruelly mocked the stilted and diffident Hirohito, who returned to Japan with a deep loathing of the arrogant European royalties, and a determination to launch his own expansive empire. But Hirohito's empire would possess a very different aim to the self-aggrandizing, competitive lust for power of the European empires of Britain, the Netherlands and France, which stretched across South-East Asia in a succession of lucrative colonies whose inhabitants had been comprehensively instilled with a recognition of the superiority of their generous colonial masters. Hirohito's empire would replace the lust for power with the lust for death: the outright obliteration and sexual crushing of entire populations in a great rush towards annihilation that would leave behind only a vastly lacerated wasteland peopled by terminally-traumatized human forms.

Hirohito was vitally supported in his aims by all of the leading figures in the Japanese military establishment, which wanted above all to subjugate itself to the imperatives of divinity embodied by Hirohito: this would then enable the military to commit whatever mass-atrocities they might wish to, in a searing rampage of glory across East Asia, without ever having to take responsibility for their acts themselves. In the five years following Hirohito's accession, the military build-up of Japan accelerated. In all of its military conflicts since the reinstitution in 1868 of the divine imperial system – in particular, its defeat of Tsarist Russia in 1905 with the naval battle of the Tsushima Straits – Japan had proved victorious, and its generals were now looking for new enemies to subdue. That military regime was torn between its envy of the European armies' readiness to devastate one another in vast spectacles of death, as they had in the recent First World War, and the need – instilled by the country's long history of intricate codes of martial honour – for Japan's military identity to be autonomous and separate from that of the armies of Europe. Japan needed to be unique and supreme: the country most ready to commit acts of torture and mass-violation on civilian populations, most eager to daringly cast off all worldwide codes and conventions of military behaviour during conflict, and most unrestrained in its desire to establish itself as the superlative authority in the will to exercise merciless totalitarian power over other countries. Only Hitler's Germany would rival Japan in these aspirations in the European sphere, and it was only natural that the two powers would eventually ally with one another.

One of the manifestations of military Japan's wholehearted commitment to cruelty was its training of young soldiers in the first years of Hirohito's regime. Although military discipline had never been lax in Japan, it was intensified to vicious levels of subjugation around the end of the 1920s. The first principle of the Japanese military was that of servitude, exacted with violence and humiliation: each rank in the military had the inalienable right to treat those in the rank below it as their slaves, and as the rankings decreased, that slavery projected itself in the kinds of acts which would become standard and mundane in the Japanese wartime internment and death-camps: anal rape, beatings with sticks and clubs, and the showering of young soldiers with verbal and literal execrations. Since the Emperor himself was the supreme leader of the Japanese military, all of those strategies of debasement, violation and beating accumulated into one divine punishment exerted by Hirohito upon his entire army, which had to respond with an attitude of adulatory servitude. Throughout Hirohito's military regime, the contrast between his lethally divine power and his actual physical presence – as a sickly weakling, shyly preoccupied with biological questions and stricken with fear whenever he was confronted with any of his imperial subjects – was starkly evident. But the military compensated for the misfortune which had given them such a dismal physical specimen for its leader (at least he was not a drooling imbecile like his short-lived father) by inciting their troops into an ever-greater state of servitude towards the living divinity who illuminated their lives. The brutal military police – the *kempeitai*, who had been instituted in 1881 but began to play an ever-more ferocious role under Hirohito, and would form a key element in overseeing his Empire's conquests – also assiduously enforced that servitude. By the beginning of the 1930s, all of Hirohito's soldiers were ready to die for him – and that death would be ecstatic, light, and a source of freedom, if it was devoted to the Emperor who had also given life to all Japanese.

Throughout the first years of Hirohito's reign, popular songs instilled in the Japanese population the sense that they were living within a constrictive space in their island of volcanic mountains, where most of the inhabitants were forced outwards to the coastlines. In the same way that Hitler was to conceive of the need and right for *Lebensraum* – expansion over the territory of weaker countries in order to give an ostensibly unique people all of the space they deserved – Hirohito and his generals began to covetously eye the entirety of China and South-East Asia. Part of Hirohito's great mission – after his humiliation at the hands of his arrogant British counterparts – was to expel the European colonial powers from East Asia, and to consolidate the entire East-Asian landmass into one block, to be controlled again by a colonial power, though this time itself an Asian one: Japan. Hirohito faced a great deal of opposition from within his political system, since his imperial power was still nominally constrained to that of a constitutional monarch. Opponents to his grand vision for expansion into East Asia had to be culled. Even in the era before he had become Emperor – when he had ruled as Regent for his mentally-incapacitated father – there had been summary killings of those who believed that Japan should not enslave and decimate its immediate neighbours in East Asia. In 1923, the leading anarchist

Sakae Osugi had been brutally killed – beaten and then lengthily throttled by the *kempeitai,* together with his wife – in the chaotic aftermath of the Tokyo earthquake of that year. A long succession of political massacres ensued, encompassing even those in central positions of power. The liberal Prime Minister Tsuyoshi Inukai, who favoured dialogue and friendship with China, was ruthlessly slaughtered by a group of naval cadets in 1932, and four years later, on 26 February 1936, the '2-26 Incident' (a future source of inspiration for the novelist Yukio Mishima's late-1960s militaristic project to create a sexually-inflected private army in total obedience to Hirohito) took place, with a group of buggery-obsessed ultra-nationalists running amok in Tokyo, arbitrarily killing cabinet ministers and attempting to assassinate the Prime Minister, before even Hirohito himself decided that they had gone too far and ordered their summary execution.

In 1931, Japan forcibly established its colonial state of Manchuria, in north-eastern China. As with many of Hitler's provocative invasions of other countries' territory, which he justified to the world by claiming that the other country had fired or tried to invade first (a strategy he employed even with Poland in September 1939), Hirohito's generals too began employing the tactic of claiming that Japan was always either responding to invitations by the people of the country it invaded, or else had been provoked into counter-attacking by a treacherous and illicit attack against it. Japan's ambitions on the mineral-rich terrain of Manchuria had already been developing for forty years: it had taken territory there in the 1890s, and its war with Tsarist Russia in 1904-5 had been largely designed to discourage Russia's own designs on the area. Japan did not immediately become involved in open warfare with China (this would not happen until six years later, after a direct confrontation between the two countries' forces near Beijing on 7 July 1937), but Manchuria was to be a crucial launching-site for Japan's onslaughts around East Asia. In China alone, the effects of the Japanese invasion would lead to the deaths of twenty million Chinese. Manchuria also constituted a prize to add to that of the territory of Korea, to the south of Manchuria, which Japan had already arbitrarily seized at the same time as its war with Russia; Manchuria also provided Japan with the space to construct its immense bacteriological extermination complex, Unit 731 (a project close to the heart of Hirohito), together with many other 'research institutes' devoted to such subjects as the elimination of syphilis from the Japanese invasion forces, who had now begun their rigorous twin-strategy of always mass-raping and then slaughtering the populations of the countries they passed through. Apart from groups of guerrilla fighters who headed for the mountains, the population of Manchuria was brutally subjugated en masse by the Japanese army and *kempeitai*, thereby becoming collective test-subjects for the medical-experimentation camps which would transform the colony, over the next fifteen years, into a bacteriologically-decimated wasteland.

After consolidating its grip on the far edge of the East-Asian mainland, Japan was ready to begin inflicting the systematic project of demented mass-extermination which Hirohito and his generals had been envisaging for the past ten years. On 14 December 1937, the Japanese army entered the large Chinese city of Nanjing, on the Yangtse river, far to the south of Manchuria. Half of the population had already fled, but enough potential victims remained for the Japanese army to stage a spectacular carnage which would definitively establish the sheer cruelty of Hirohito's regime to the entire world. The soldiers and *kempeitai* agents immediately began the killing of everyone who had remained in the city streets, bayonet-charging and decapitating the population in a great cacophony of triumphant screams, torn flesh and victims' cries. For the next six weeks, they conducted one of the most headlong and sustained atrocity-campaigns of the twentieth-century, careering around the city's streets night after night, crazed with alcohol, breaking into the terrified inhabitants' houses and multiply-raping almost all of the city's female population, regardless of age. A high proportion of the inhabitants of Nanjing who had been violated were also killed: they were either repeatedly bayoneted (a few women managed to survive this) or were locked into warehouses in crowded groups by the Japanese soldiers and then incinerated. By the beginning of January 1938, Nanjing was a city of the dead, with vast piles of putrefying corpses lining the streets. The river had

Nanjing – victims of mass slaughter

been used as a dumping ground for the butchered citizens, until the riverbed itself had become so saturated with human carcasses that the Japanese troops could safely walk across its surface from bank to bank. By the time the Japanese were ready to head off for their next destination, over 250,000 inhabitants of Nanjing had been slaughtered. The general in charge of the Japanese forces, Iwane Matsui (who would eventually be hanged as a war criminal), announced: 'Now the flag of the Rising Sun is floating high over Nanjing, and the Imperial Way is shining... The dawn of the renaissance of the East is on the verge of appearing.'

Even Hitler was awed by the scale of the butchery at Nanjing, and ordered the atrocity to be condemned as the 'criminal acts' of a 'bestial machinery'. But he was deeply impressed by the sheer ferocity and application of Hirohito's divine will, and soon instructed his Embassies in East Asia to recognise the legitimacy of Japan's berserk rampage across China's territory. In many ways, the

Nanjing – bayoneting live prisoners

decimation of Nanjing – whose effects were extensively filmed and shown worldwide as newsreel spectacles – became Japan's media-manifesto to the colonial powers of Europe that their ostensibly-benign and haphazard regimes had become abruptly archaic, and would imminently be supplanted by the ferocity of Hirohito's 'maximum-strength' colonial systems, which operated on new principles of mass-subjugation, all-out butchery and sexual servitude. This was in stark contrast to the British approach of extracting as much wealth from their colonies as possible while congratulating themselves that they were demonstrating compassionate humanity to their fortunate colonial subjects. And

Nanjing – prisoners buried alive

it was even further away from the still-more self-delusional approach of the French, who – in their East-Asian colonial 'protectorates' such as Cambodia and Vietnam – were convinced that they were magnanimously imparting a profound sense of civilization and culture to their dominions, whose aristocrats and intellectuals were often ingratiatingly complicit with their colonizers. Now, Japan had introduced a new form of malevolently-viral and destructive colonial power into the smoothly-running European system – one which would contribute to the shattering and expulsion of all of the European colonial powers over the next twenty years.

Nanjing – victim garrotted, with eyes gouged out

For the young Japanese troops themselves, their routine of murderous onslaughts from city to city across the eastern edges of China formed a time of glory. Although the low-ranking soldiers remained in constant danger of being violently humiliated by their military superiors for a range of infractions (such as not being sufficiently deadly in their bayonet charges), they had the compensation of possessing an ultimate liberty to mete out whatever acts of gratuitous slaughter or sexual violation to their victims that they desired, and then being able (assuming they were ever to be asked to justify themselves, which in almost all cases never happened) to provide the supreme validation for their acts that they had been done while 'fighting for the Emperor', who encouraged his forces to 'work diligently' for the future of China under his imperial rule, and demonstrated a keen interest in the results of the air-attacks with biological weaponry, inflicted on urban populations along the seaboard of China, that were now being organized by the research-units which had been established across Japan's new territory. Every victory by the Japanese army was followed by its dedication in a mass shout ('*Banzai!*') to Hirohito himself. The only deficit in Japan's murderous incursion into China was that the vast territory was almost impossible to fully subdue, and many troops who were engaged in its forcible occupation would soon need to be transferred further down the East Asian mainland to take part in securing the next targets in Hirohito's colonial designs.

As Japan's hold on China deepened, the imperial troops developed ever-greater skill in mutilating the still-living bodies of their victims, whom they massacred in their hundreds of thousands at every available opportunity. As the years went by, the death toll of Chinese victims extended into the millions. On the frontier between Manchuria and the Soviet Union, small-scale skirmishes occasionally took place between the Japanese and Soviet troops, and any infrequent prisoners taken (on either side) were exhaustively tortured and mutilated, before being slaughtered and their bodies returned to their own forces. In one incident in December 1938, the Japanese captured a young Soviet lieutenant who had been stranded behind the Japanese lines during the desultory skirmishing around the border. A rare Soviet captive, in contrast to the endless millions of Chinese, provided the opportunity for 'special treatment', in the form of adroit and sustained mutilation. The Japanese troops carefully carved five stars into his back, and then a larger star, together with the hammer-and-sickle emblem of

Chinese war poster depicting Japanese atrocities

Stalin's regime, into his chest. The lieutenant's feet were set on fire until they turned black, and his fingernails wrenched out with pliers. Bullet cartridges were then hammered into each of the lieutenant's eyes and the bones in his wrists and ankles were shattered with rifle-butts. His ears were sliced off and his tongue pulled out by the roots. The Japanese then rammed a large anti-tank shell into the lieutenant's anus (finally killing him) and sliced off his penis, before inviting his comrades, who had been listening to his agonized screams on the far side of the frontier, to come and collect him. The Japanese troops' awareness that similar mutilations might well await them if they were to be captured by their enemies increased their determination never to surrender during the conflicts which they had unleashed across East Asia, and always to die joyfully on the battle-field in order never to betray their Emperor.

By 1940, Hirohito had instigated a new regime for the East Asian mainland, and was ready to extend it southwards. Although Japan and the Soviet Union remained at glaring loggerheads on their frontier, with small-scale occasional eruptions, it was a static face-off for the time being. The advantages to be gained from the Japanese perspective in invading the Soviet Union were negligibly slight, since to the north of Manchuria lay the terminal hell of eastern Siberia – with temperatures at seventy to eighty degrees celsius below zero and total darkness for much of the year – where, in deep secrecy, Stalin was disposing of millions of his own troublesome enemies, in the vast complex of death-camps around Magadan, nine hundred miles to the north of Manchuria. While Stalin's regime was preoccupied in exterminating many millions of its starving, frozen and sexual-slavery subjugated victims in the annihilation zone of Magadan, Hirohito's troops were assiduously mutilating, raping and massacring millions of their Chinese colonial subjects from their base in Manchuria, and extending their grip on China southwards. Both too busy – for the time being – with their respective works of mass-extermination, Hirohito and Stalin contemptuously ignored one another and continued with their great projects.

The alliance between Hitler's Germany and Hirohito's Japan finally came to fruition on 27 September 1940, with the signing of agreements in Tokyo and Berlin (Japan also found itself allied with the more-lacklustre Italy in the 'Tripartite Alliance'). Hitler had already been at war with Britain and other western European countries for over a year, and had already overturned two of the great colonial powers of South-East Asia, France and the Netherlands, whose territories were now up for grabs. Having the ferocious power of Germany alongside Japan would consolidate Hirohito's imperial mission to decimate the entirety of South-East Asia with impunity, and his generals intensified their plans to burst through all of the colonial boundaries of Britain, as well as the already-ripped territories of France and the Netherlands, thereby unleashing extreme regimes of terror and comprehensively subjugating the entirety of East Asia's populations under the control of Japan. However, Japan faced a new challenge in the USA's decision to oppose its occupation of China (where Japan had regularly attacked American citizens, property and shipping), threatening blockades and embargoes that would obstruct Japan's access to the necessary raw materials for its imminent invasions – oil, minerals and metals – unless it withdrew from China. From Japan, the threats of the US President Franklin D. Roosevelt were seen as a gratuitous provocation (whereas from the US, they were seen as a reasonable ultimatum), and a new escalation began of the dominant world powers' descent into an all-engulfing conflict – a conflict that formed an enticing new challenge for Japan to become involved in, even if it were to obliterate itself in the process and disappear into terminal oblivion as a result. The onset of war between Japan and the USA (together with Britain) would also provide a suitable impetus for Japan to begin its long-awaited murderous sweep down the South-East Asian coastline towards Britain's colonies. After reflection (and a degree of intricate in-fighting among the Japanese military leaders and politicians, including Hirohito's new Prime Minister, Hideki Tojo), Hirohito and his generals duly decided that the best option would be a pre-emptive strike on the crucial US naval-base at Pearl Harbor in Hawaii, and on 7 December 1941, after many months of preparation, Japan's massed air-squadrons headed east across the Pacific Ocean to decimate the USA's Pearl Harbor fleet, while its other forces were streaming headlong southwards towards the British centres of colonial power in Hong Kong and Singapore.

UNIT 731: HUMAN WIPEOUT

While Japan was extending its Empire of headlong slaughter across China and planning its further expansion throughout the entirety of South-East Asia and beyond, a unique city of death evolved within its new territory of Manchuria, operating largely in autonomy from the turmoil surrounding it. This was Unit 731, Japan's great centre of experimentation and innovation into the nature of death and the extremities of the human body. At Unit 731, the biological warfare trials, dissections and eviscerations of living prisoners, and crucifixions of captured prisoners of war, all contributed to Japan's vast project for the mass extermination of its enemies. That regime of extermination extended far beyond the rampaging bayonet-charges and lethal sexual violations of entire populations which had been brutally inflicted upon the massacred inhabitants of Nanjing and other Chinese cities; Japan's regime of obliteration also encompassed more sophisticated, methodical explorations into probing the point at which the substance of human life itself could be strategically torn apart and made to implode backwards into the malevolent raw material of its seething bacterial components. Unit 731 belonged firmly within the Japanese medical tradition of investigating the science of death to its very boundaries. As soon as Manchuria had fallen to Japan in 1931, Hirohito and his generals commanded that this new part of the Empire – with its endless millions of potential test-subjects ready for systematic corporeal experimentation – would form the perfect annihilation-zone for an invaluable programme of unprecedented research (one which could be looked back upon with pride for generations to come) into the extreme limits of the human body under intensive torture, sexual subjugation and neural obliteration via biological attacks. All of the financial and scientific resources of the Empire were immediately put at the disposal of the ambitious biologist appointed by Hirohito to head Unit 731, Shiro Ishii, who was to pursue his imperially-appointed duties with obsessional zeal and commitment to the very end. At Unit 731, all conceptions of the human body itself would be erased and reformulated from scratch.

The location chosen for Unit 731 was in the vicinity of the Manchurian city of Harbin. The first complex built to house the thousands of scientists and their test-subjects proved to be located too close to the city (attracting the attention of the local inhabitants) and was soon demolished; the final location – Pingfang – was situated further out from Harbin, though still close to the railway and road networks which were essential for supplying vast quantities of experimental test-subjects. An airfield was also constructed alongside the complex so that the scientists could easily travel to Tokyo and back in order to receive and execute the orders of Hirohito and his generals. As well as the inhabitants of the surrounding cities, the population of Unit 731 would also include captured Chinese resistance fighters who were attempting to drive back the Japanese onslaught, together with large numbers of Russians who were fleeing Stalin's purges and had crossed the border into north-eastern China (believing that they had escaped into safety), prisoners from Japan's more long-established colony of Korea, to the south of Manchuria, and, finally, once the Second World War had begun, a scattering of mainly US and British PoWs who were transferred to Unit 731 for 'special treatment'. Unit 731 was a vast city of annihilation in its own right, with the brick buildings extending over several square miles: luxurious, centrally-heated villas and recreation centres for the scientists, barracks for the Japanese troops who corralled the test-subjects and guarded the complex (along with eager recruits from some of the countries already incorporated into Japan's Empire, such as Taiwan), accommodation in the form of great prison-blocks for the test-subjects, and – most important of all – the labyrinthine network of laboratories, dissection rooms and incineration chambers which comprised the core of the immense complex. By 1939, Unit 731 was fully operational. It had been built to last: the Emperor had decreed that its work should continue, with ever-greater determination, for many generations; as a result, the brick-constructed buildings were reinforced with steel-supported concrete. Towering above Unit 731, two enormous chimneys were constructed in order to diffuse the often-toxic ashes of its victims far into the sky so that they would not infect the complex's own scientists.

The scientist charged with running Unit 731, Shiro Ishii, was known throughout his new domain as 'The Boss'. Ishii, who was born in 1892, had been the most brilliant and obsessionally single-minded student of his generation at the Kyoto Imperial University, where the study of bacteriology had been pioneered with the original aim of providing an antiseptic environment for surgical operations. Even as a student, Ishii had been contemptuous of such mundane practices. He rapidly rose to prominence in the deeply-hierarchical Japanese medical

establishment with his innovative theories of how bacterial and germ-warfare could be used as a strategy of 'human wipeout' in order to further the Empire's territorial ambitions (as well as making a vital and prestigious contribution to scientific knowledge). Ishii had soon amassed hundreds of young acolytes among the medical profession, and many of them would follow their mentor to the grim colony of Manchuria in the late 1930s. In the early 1920s, there had still been opposition to Ishii from doctors who believed that bacteriological science should be intended only to preserve life, but these dissidents often found themselves being covertly assassinated by Ishii's acolytes. And once Hirohito – who always took a close interest in medical matters, especially dissection – had become Emperor in 1926, Ishii's career soared. Ishii was always eager to impress the Emperor with his well-documented discoveries at Unit 731, and had many of his experiments filmed. The 16mm films, shot by specially-trained Unit 731 guards, were dispatched to the Imperial Palace in Tokyo for the Emperor himself to avidly view. A distant cousin of the Emperor, the minor prince Takeda no Miya (who would later become one of the principal organizers of the Tokyo Olympic Games in 1964), worked at Unit 731 and was often charged with delivering the reels of film to Hirohito. He recalled: 'I remember the times when I had to deliver the Boss's [Ishii's] briefcase to the Imperial Household. I was taken there in an official car with a driver, the Unit leader's flag on the fender. I was just a young man, and yet the guard gave me a respectful salute when I handed him the briefcase. It had cans of 16mm films, records of the Boss's experiments, and its destination was an imperial conference.' The Imperial Palace archives in Tokyo still contain many thousands of locked-away reels of film-footage from Unit 731's atrocities.

Ishii ruthlessly ran Unit 731 (whose name had been chosen by Ishii in 1941 to allow its unique experiments to temporarily vanish in anonymity within the work of the many other Japanese death-oriented research units of the time, until the moment came for its glory to be revealed to the world); new railway lines were built on Ishii's orders right across Japan's territory in southern and eastern China so that he would never be short of test-subjects for his imperially-sanctioned great work. Soon, Unit 731 was smoothly operating as what Ishii referred to as a 'killing machine', capable of inflicting tens of thousands of deaths within its own walls each month, together with hundreds of thousands of deaths – via the results of its bacteriological experiments – upon the urban populations of the Chinese cities. Even that monumental and rigorously-sustained death-toll was viewed only as a first stage by Ishii, who had been invested with the sacred imperial duty of devising a suitable means for the mass-extermination of all of Japan's enemies, which – once the Second World War had begun – also encompassed the USA, Britain and Australia. Ishii's dedicated scientists worked nineteen-hour days throughout the end of the 1930s and right up to the summer of 1945; their only relaxation, in the recreation halls attached to the complex, came at the expert hands of the sex-slave Russian prisoners of Unit 731, many of whom were statuesque white-blonde women of exquisite beauty, who had fled their homes in western Siberia in order to escape the wrath of Stalin and had now ended up servicing the lusts of salivating Japanese doctors whom they comprehensively dwarfed with their immense height.

The prisoners at Unit 731 were known by their guards as 'the logs'; when the curious Chinese inhabitants of the region had first asked the Japanese soldiers what they were doing in their immense complex, they had jokingly replied that they were 'collecting logs', and the prisoners themselves soon began to be contemptuously called 'the logs' – always ready to be stacked into great heaps and then burned. (In the same idiom, Stalin would often wise-crack that the inmates of his own death-camps were called 'railway sleepers', since so many thousands of them expired from overwork and exposure while building the immense railway lines that brought the prisoners intended for execution to their places of death on the frozen perimeters of his Empire.) The Chinese inhabitants of the Harbin region often became included among the experimental test-subjects of Unit 731, but many hundreds of others were also employed by Ishii to undertake the menial tasks that needed to be done there, such as the collection and disposal of the vast containers of internal organs and emptied-out bodies of the test-subjects. Ishii was keen to keep the running-costs of Unit 731 down to an absolute minimum, and he instituted a regime by which the Chinese workers were paid only in high-quality heroin (which was produced in vast quantities at other Japanese research units across Manchuria); this narcotic regime had the dual benefits of transforming the Chinese into compliant workers who were always prepared to commit any atrocity or dispose of its evidence in order to receive their 'payment', and also served to give them a supremely oblivious frame of mind which allowed them to pursue their duties without being distracted. The Japanese soldiers also liked to joke to the Chinese population of the region that Unit 731 was a 'water-purification plant'. The prisoners themselves were kept relatively well-fed until it was their turn to enter the experimentation blocks; the Japanese appreciated the value of having healthy test-subjects, and although the prisoners were kept caged in vast dormitories of minuscule wire containers – placed ten-deep, one on top of the other, so that excrement and urine habitually rained down on those in the lower tiers – they were always provided with several bowls of rice each day, supplemented by cubes of raw meat sliced from the now-moribund bodies of the previous generation of prisoners.

One of the primary uses of those prisoners who were not earmarked for dissection at Unit 731 was to be subjected to plague experiments. The prisoners were crowded together into great empty hangars infested with starving, plague-bearing rats and with fleas which had been feeding on the blood of the rats. The doctors then calculated the amount of time it took for all of the prisoners to be bitten by the rats and fleas, before contracting plague and expiring in outright agony; these experiments assisted Ishii's staff in their attempts to design ever-purer variants of plague which could decimate their victims in the shortest possible time. The rats were infected with plague by being given injections and then placed in glass jars, each equipped with an opening through which vast numbers of fleas could then feed on their blood by sucking it out through incisions in the rats' stomachs. The wide-scale practical application of Ishii's experiments in the world outside Unit 731 took the form of the droppings by planes of thousands of plague-bearing fleas on those Chinese cities which had still not been completely subjugated by the Japanese forces, such as Ningbo and Hangzhou, both of which were repeatedly attacked by air-assaults of killer-fleas in 1940 and 1941. The Japanese preferred to concentrate their plague-attacks on port cities, since these possessed the greatest strategic importance in Japan's great imperial conquest of the South-East Asian landmass. Hundreds of thousands of Chinese civilians contracted plague (a lethally-mutated variant of bubonic plague, intended to act rapidly and with optimum results) after seeing the hovering Japanese planes drop dense clouds of fleas onto their cities. Many of the Chinese could not understand what was happening to them and believed that they must have been cursed by their deities, who had formed malevolent alliances with the all-powerful Japanese hordes. The city streets soon became filled with thousands of victims whose faces had turned purple-black. Their glands swelled up to the size of balloons and their overheated bodies soared to white-hot temperatures, finally expelling their internal fluids and liquefied organs out through their anal and other orifices in great high-pressure ejaculations of vivid yellow and purple matter. The victims, in extreme agony, raked their own faces with their fingernails, tearing their flesh apart and extracting their own eyes into their stiffening fists. After a series of bone-shattering convulsions, the plague-victims would then abruptly expire. Very few inhabitants survived or managed to evade the plague-fleas. After receiving reports of the initial success of his experiments, Ishii ordered that they should now be inflicted on an ever-wider scale, and his covert hit-squads travelled by road and rail as well as by air, to infiltrate the Chinese cities and unleash their plague-fleas. As well as cities which remained under the control of the Chinese army, cities within Manchuria itself and the territory seized in 1937 by the Japanese forces were also systematically infected, once their contingents of occupying troops had been evacuated. Some of the cities were so thoroughly infected with Ishii's 'premium-grade' plague that they remained subject to new outbreaks of the ineradicable disease sixty years later. Ishii also experimented with decimating entire urban populations with anthrax, and worked on spreading other diseases, such as cholera, typhoid and 'rotten-leg' disease (a Unit 731 'speciality' in which the victim's arms and legs progressively putrefied and turned black, causing intense pain, until they fell off, leaving behind only a limbless trunk of rancid flesh); however, nothing proved so exhaustively lethal as Ishii's urban plague-attacks. By 1943, between two and three million urban Chinese had expired in torment as a result of the Unit 731 experiments.

Within the confines of Unit 731 itself, Ishii was also hard at work on other projects. Although Japan was not yet at war with the Soviet Union (whose leader, Stalin, bluntly dismissed the divine Hirohito as a 'midget-cretin'), the Emperor had instructed Ishii to devise experiments that would enable Japanese troops to survive the icy wastelands of Siberia, in the event that the Empire might want to expand northwards. Japan had easily defeated the then still-Tsarist Russia in the countries' war of 1904-5, and Hirohito – for whom the victory celebrations were a cherished early-childhood memory – was confident that Stalin's domain would prove to be an equally shoddy adversary for Japan. The biologically-inclined Hirohito was also considering being cryogenically frozen after death, in order that he would be able to reawaken from time to time in order to ensure that future Emperors rigorously pursued and consolidated his own obliterating victories over the subjugated peoples of South-East Asia. As a result, Ishii systematically experimented with inflicting extreme cold on his prisoners and carefully recorded the results. Among Unit 731's most massive buildings was a reinforced refrigeration block (so solidly built that it survived the end of the war, only partially ruined by the attempts to demolish it, and still stands on the site of the death-complex); the block contained a series of massive chambers for the freezing of large groups of prisoners, and also individual cells allocated for special experiments. Ishii's staff calculated the exact moment at which the human body froze to a lethal level of immobility and its flesh began to glacify. In order to discover the extent to which the prisoners' internal organs had also frozen, their bodies were gradually chipped-apart with hammers, often while still alive, until they formed piles of ice-and-bone debris on the refrigeration unit's concrete floor. In order to test the impact of weapons on bodies in a frozen state, the guards would also violently club the groups of iced prisoners with iron bars, sending cracked-off limbs flying in all directions and immediately decapitating the test-subjects, their facial features immobilized into a terminal rictus of terror and agony that, for its observers, appeared to convey pleasure and even ecstasy at their refrigeration.

After the beginning of the Second World War and the capturing of large numbers of American, British and Australian prisoners of war, Ishii eagerly ordered supplies of PoWs to be delivered to Unit 731 to take part in his experiments; he was convinced that the prisoners would understand that they were participating in some of the most innovative medical trials ever devised. The strategy of testing the bodies of prisoners from countries which Japan was fighting against had its evident advantages, since Ishii had been instructed by Hirohito to develop systems of eradication suitable for application to American and European populations, and the PoWs' levels of resistance against the diseases to which they were subjected would help Ishii plan for the future mass-obliteration attacks that were envisaged. Many of these experiments on Allied PoWs were staged at a death-facility annex to Unit 731, at Anda, located eighty miles to the south of the main complex. Ishii ordered the prisoners to be crucified in large circles of forty men – the arrangements being carefully recorded by his staff in drawings – and then ordered his planes to fly low overhead and to drop lethal concoctions of bacterial weapons in small, concentrated amounts, in order to gauge how quickly they would lead to the demise of the prisoners, who were kept in a state of acute mental and corporeal tension and alertness by the act of crucifixion. Each PoW was numbered so that his individual responses to the diseases unleashed could be assessed. Ishii's doctors had to be careful to remain at a safe distance and downwind of the experiments, in order not to be infected themselves (even so, a number of Ishii's staff succumbed to glorious deaths in their imperial service, after sudden changes of wind direction). Although Ishii considered the results of these experiments to be of vital importance, in measuring the ways in which different bacteriological weapons functioned and could be combined into ever-deadlier variants against Japan's enemies, he was never able to receive the large quantities of PoWs he demanded from their internment camps in Singapore and Borneo, since their new masters had other urgent uses for them.

Ishii's greatest source of pride at Unit 731 – apart from his plague-attacks, refrigeration-trials and mass-crucifixions of Allied PoWs – was his corporeal experiments. This was the work closest to his heart, for which he fully expected to receive the Nobel Prize and other prestigious honours. Ishii's project was to use the human body as a bacterial hothouse, injecting it with combinations of the most virulent diseases and allowing them to develop, before collecting the cultivated germs just as they developed to their maximum virulence, by dissecting and eviscerating their human 'hosts' while they were still alive; the empty body could then be left to die. The dissected organs that were excess to requirements were simply tossed into buckets on the floor and left for the heroin-abusing Chinese assistants to collect and incinerate, along with the voided bodies, which always burned-up rapidly because of their emptiness. Many of the most annihilatory bacteriological concoctions developed by Ishii – which were tested out to discover their levels of lethal effect by dropping them from planes on the Chinese cities – were discovered in this way. Over the years that Unit 731 was in operation, tens of thousands of test-subjects passed through Ishii's dissection rooms, where the surgical teams worked in relays, twenty-four hours a day. Those who could operate with supreme speed and skill were known as the 'dissection wizards'. Ishii himself personally supervised many of the experiments. From time to time, Ishii's 'dissection wizards' also went on tours around the Manchurian countryside, arbitrarily seizing peasants and dissecting them in the open air. They would also make sudden appearances in the Chinese cities that had been ravaged by plague-attacks, after the contaminated air had cleared, and select agonized victims (preferably those who were still alive) to eviscerate on the spot. All of the bodies of test-subjects who had revealed unusual or enlightening results under dissection – the 'special-category specimens', as they were called – were sent back to Tokyo by air, and examined at Ishii's secondary research unit there, in the district of Shinjuku, so that the most interesting data could immediately be transmitted to the Emperor himself. The bodies were then finally buried in the grounds of the Tokyo unit, which would later be entirely destroyed in the Tokyo firestorms of March 1945. (During building-excavation work in Shinjuku in 1998, many of the skeletal remains of the 'special-category' victims of Unit 731 were unearthed.) The Unit 731 chimneys, working under the cover of darkness, pumped the still-deadly ashes of the test-subjects high into the air above the complex.

One of Ishii's favourite occupations in the dissection rooms at Unit 731 was to conduct interviews with the 'bodies-without-organs'. The prisoners were chloroformed into immobile semi-consciousness on their arrival in the dissection room, but, once most of their internal organs had been removed, the chloroform would wear off and they would re-awaken to discover that they had been comprehensively eviscerated. At first, they would attempt to scream, but then became quiet and receptive to questioning, in the minutes before they fell into a terminal coma. Ishii's poignant interviews were recorded in his documentation of the experiments. Via an interpreter, he would ask them: 'How do you feel? What is it like to be alive without organs?'. The prisoners would sometimes become agitated and ask about the fate of their families, but others were more resigned and replied: 'I feel fine. Without organs, life is better. My body feels better. I feel as though I could do anything now, travel anywhere I wished, through time and space...'.

Although the sexual torture of the Unit 731 test-subjects was not a top priority for the dedicated Ishii (mass-extermination was his sacred goal), he allowed his guards a certain degree of levity to commit acts of sexual atrocity on the prisoners, as long as they excluded those who were destined to take part in his dissection experiments. The guards had began to realise – especially in the war's final years – that they were in increasing danger of being themselves subjected to appropriately harsh reprisals, either from the Chinese themselves or from one of Japan's enemy powers, and Ishii was eager not to see them mutiny and destroy his work before its glorious completion. Ishii also allowed his guards to make occasional 'recreational' forays outside Unit 731, and they conducted headlong terror-rampages, inflicting mass-decapitations on all of the peasants they could find, and then entering the nearby towns to sexually abuse and massacre their entire populations before setting the towns on fire. By the closing days of Unit 731, the area immediately around it had been thoroughly pillaged and its inhabitants slaughtered, so that the great death-city of Unit 731 stood isolated within a largely depopulated zone of smoking, corpse-strewn fields, and of emptied, flame-blackened towns.

As the war went on, the Emperor's appeals for Ishii to decimate the cities of his enemies became increasingly frantic. Ishii now possessed vast quantities of bacteriological weapons that were capable of carrying through the obliteration of the USA's entire population forty times over, and he desperately tried to devise a means of transporting his killer-fleas to the American cities. He worked out an intricate plan by which the populations of those cities would all be simultaneously exterminated through the application of a deadly combination of plague and anthrax. The only obstacle to his grand scheme was that the mainland of the USA was never within range of Japanese air-assaults during the conflict. As Hirohito's empire of slaughter began to disintegrate, Ishii knew that he had failed in his great work of disseminating the imperial 'service to humanity' of Unit 731 to the world at large. His long-developed philosophy of systematic human annihilation had been prevented from being put fully into action only by the sheer distance that stretched between Unit 731's massed ranks of imperial fleas, already infected with their pay-load of plague, and their just-out-of-reach enemies. Faced with this devastating setback, Ishii could only re-double his dissection-room experiments into exploring the extreme boundaries of the human body in its collision with death.

THE ANAL RAPE AND CRUCIFIXION OF ALLIED POWs

Once imperial Japan's forces had been unleashed down the face of South-East

Asia, in the aftermath of Hirohito's great victory at Pearl Harbor on 7 December 1941, the intensity of the will to inflict mass-torture and extermination on blameless civilian populations increased to unstoppable levels of ferocity. The second phase of Hirohito's grand plan had now been put into operation: after South-East Asia had been completely cast into servitude, his forces could link up with those of Hitler to lay waste to the USA and any other remaining pockets of resistance to the worldwide totalitarian dominion that was to be arbitrarily shared-out between Hitler, Hirohito and the verbose Italian dictator Benito Mussolini. Then, the real work of annihilation could begin. As soon as it became evident that the colonial British and their armies were to be no match for the rampaging hordes of Hirohito, a massive rush began among the young inhabitants of Japan to join their Emperor's invincible army and take part in the magnificent subjugation of South-East Asia. All of the cities of Japan were largely emptied of men between the ages of sixteen and forty as they became rapidly channelled into the momentum of Japan's powerful push southwards. The country's rural population, too – adept in the use of machetes and fully-accustomed already, from their lives in the countryside, to a pitiless day-to-day regime comprising of bestiality, sexual violation and incest – abruptly left their fields, from Kyushu in the south to Hokkaido in the north, and hurried to participate in Japan's moment of supreme glory.

One of Hirohito's principal targets was Singapore, which had been a British colony for over a century and whose strategic position, at the far southern tip of the Malay peninsula, controlled all access to the territories of South-East Asia. The assault on Singapore began at the same moment as the victory at Pearl Harbor had been achieved, and the colony was rapidly subjugated in the following month, January 1942, after minimal resistance and negligible losses for the Japanese forces. The vast British army stationed in Singapore, along with many thousands of troops from its colonial possessions, became terrified as Japan's mighty forces rampaged inexorably towards them down the entire length of the narrow Malay peninsula; the British generals started to panic and their troops deserted in large numbers, looking for places to hide. Finally, the generals

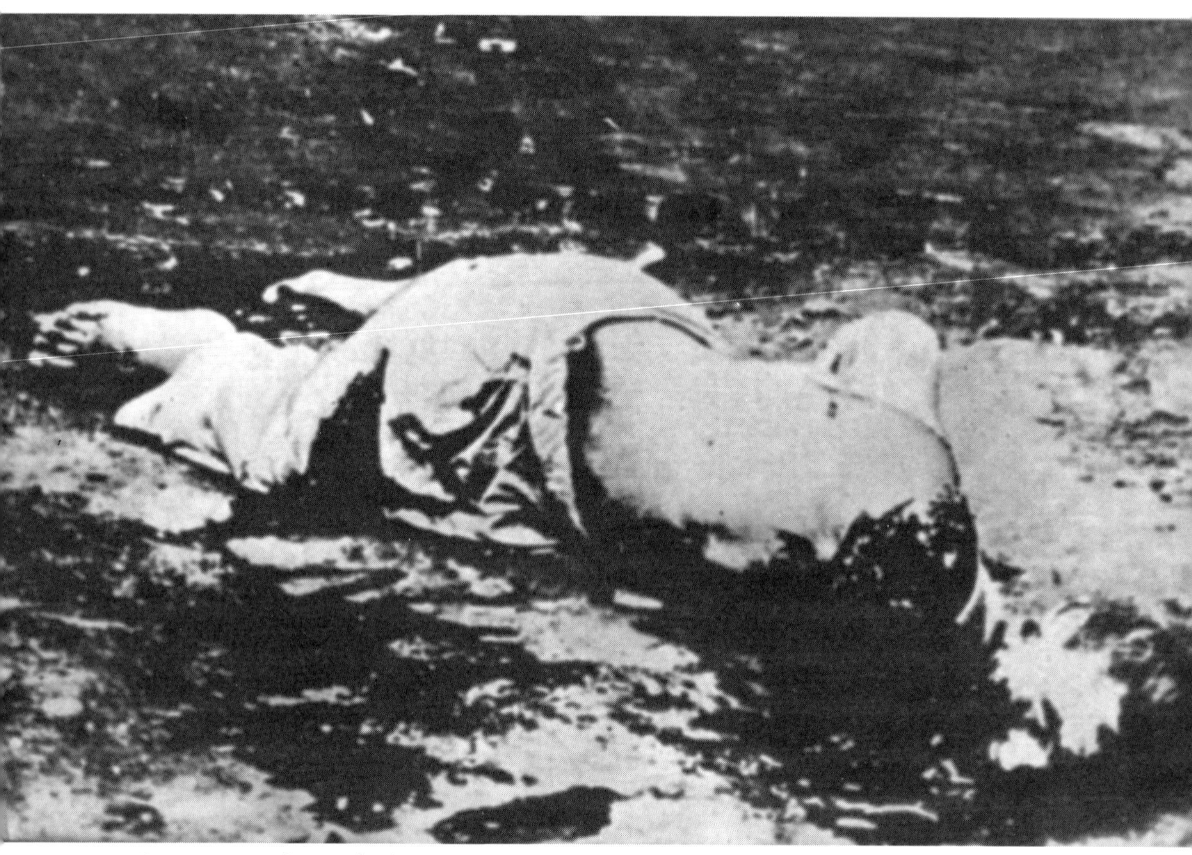

Singapore – victim decapitated in the street

decided that the most courageous plan for the British was to surrender unconditionally to the far smaller Japanese forces without a fight, and seventy thousand British troops, together with another ninety thousand colonial soldiers, were delivered-up to the astonished Japanese, who immediately began to devise means for the utilization and summary disposal of this unexpected corporeal bonanza. The surrendered troops – many of whom, only weeks before, had been employed in the factories and dockyards of provincial Britain – now sat in an endless ocean of docile human flesh as they awaited the caprices of their new owners. Meanwhile, the Japanese violently subjugated Singapore itself with the same kinds of tactics they had successfully pioneered in Nanjing four years earlier, with the mass-killing and sexual violation of the civilian population, in a generalized frenzy of exhilarated carnage. Particular attention was given to committing acts of gratuitous slaughter in hospitals, where doctors and nurses were stopped in mid-operation and mercilessly culled, together with the patients they were in the process of operating upon. Soon, the cityscape of Singapore was in flames. The elderly British Prime Minister, Winston Churchill, who spent almost the entirety of the war years in bed, issuing orders to his secretaries in a chronic drunken stupor punctuated by deafening bouts of flatulence, heard the news of the Fall of Singapore with deep dismay; already a consumer of three bottles of premium-strength Armenian brandy (specially supplied to him by his ally Stalin) each day, Churchill's response was to order an extra bottle and to morosely slur: 'This is our darkest hour.'

Over the next three months, the unstoppable momentum of the Japanese forces led to the violent overrunning of almost the entirety of South-East Asia; once they had subjugated Singapore and Hong Kong (another highly-prized British colony), together with Malaya, Sumatra, Borneo and New Guinea, only the Arafura Sea would separate them from the less-than-prestigious British colonial dominion of Australia, whose blighted shores even the fanatically territory-seizing Japanese were reluctant to occupy. However, the occupation of Manila – the capital of the Philippines (the large archipelago which had been an American colony since 1898) – was undertaken by the Japanese with devastating cruelty and a thorough-going regime of atrocities exacted on the civilian population, in a sustained operation of butchery and rape which would continue unabated for the next three years. As the unwilling colonial subjects of the USA, the Philippino population now became liable to a special level of mass-extermination and sexual violation at the hands of the victory-crazed Japanese troops, whose supreme commander demanded that the resistant inhabitants of Manila should be reduced to a level of utter servitude or else economically obliterated. The order was issued: 'When eliminating Philippinos, assemble them together in one place, as far as possible, thereby saving ammunition and labour. The disposal of dead bodies will be troublesome, so either collect them in houses scheduled to be burned or throw them in the river.' In the Philippines, the Japanese also managed to capture enormous numbers of American troops, who had been abandoned by their hapless commander, General Douglas MacArthur, on the

Borneo – death sculpture

Bataan peninsula, and ordered to surrender unconditionally to the approaching Japanese hordes. The sheer number of prisoners (at least seventy-five thousand on the Bataan peninsula alone) placed an excessive strain on their Japanese captors, who had not been expecting such eager capitulations, and they decided to efficiently shrink the number of prisoners by sending them on a sixty-five-mile death-march, without water or food, in extreme temperatures. Along the way, the prisoners were randomly decapitated as they marched, and the Japanese also disposed of some of the vast human excess by running tanks over them, leaving behind flattened human exclamation-marks of oozing scarlet pulp on the road. But the most effective strategy discovered by the Japanese for reducing the number of their prisoners was to halt the march at isolated spots and order the soldiers to bury one another alive; they were formed into human queues of death, with one screaming prisoner being buried in a pit while another four covered him over with spadefuls of ochre mud. Any prisoners who refused to participate in the scheme were summarily decapitated or else fast-tracked to the front of the queue for immediate burial.

Philippines — bones of executed US soldiers

In all of the colonial territories in South-East Asia seized by the Japanese during the first half of 1942, a top-priority was to capture and massacre any of the colonial masters who had not already escaped or been evacuated by their governments. The power of the European countries – Britain, the Netherlands, France and Portugal – which owned colonies in South-East Asia had been effortlessly swept aside, either by the Japanese themselves, or by their German allies who had already overrun the French and Dutch centres of colonial power in Europe itself. But, especially in the case of Britain, the colonies were run by die-hards who regarded the Japanese forces as beyond contempt and their divine Emperor as a myopic midget; as a result, the intransigent colonials were often still ensconced in their salubrious villas on their vast plantations, being fanned or fellated by their 'number-two' boys, as the Japanese arrived. In many cases, the captured colonials were then removed from their plantations and publicly executed en masse, hung upside-down in the palm-shaded colonial city-squares and summarily hacked to pieces with machete blows by the glowering Japanese troops, as they maintained their outraged dignity to the end, spluttering their disdain for the 'monkeys' who had dispossessed them of their own divine right to their colonial domains. The European colonies in South-East Asia would never recover from their upturning by the Japanese, who intended to set up their own colonial empire of outright slaughter and permanent subjugation.

By the spring of 1942, the Japanese had established the extreme limits of that South-East Asian empire; still half-heartedly contemplating the unenticing prospect of invading Australia, they had now seized the entirety of the mineral-rich territories of the region, and were consolidating the vast expanse of their new imperial annexations by slaughtering and enslaving their populations (many of whom were thoroughly complicit in the Japanese scheme, while others – such as the islanders of New Guinea – would tenaciously resist their subjugation). But it soon became apparent that the Japanese had overstretched themselves in their ambition for devastating carnage and territorial acquisition. Even with the massive influx of dedicated young recruits into its army, there were simply not enough Japanese to sustain such a vast empire, and inadequate supply-lines to keep it smoothly functioning. As a result, the conflict reached a stalemate during the middle of 1942, with the two sets of leaders glaring both at their adversaries and also suspiciously eyeing their allies for signs of treachery. On one side, there was the divine Hirohito and his Prime Minister Hideki Tojo, together with Hitler and his leather-clad sidekick, the Italian dictator Mussolini; and on the other side, the addled Churchill, Stalin and the American President Roosevelt, who all fiercely detested one another. Until the massive industrial force and resources of the USA started gradually to turn the conflict in its favour, the worldwide balance of power between the two factions became frozen into immobility, with all space and time sucked into a malevolent black void, within which the Japanese forces were at liberty to exact an unparalleled regime of supreme cruelty and sexual atrocity upon their enslaved colonial subjects, and most especially upon their hundreds of thousands of prisoners of war.

In the Allied soldiers' enthusiastic rush – in their hundreds of thousands – to be enslaved as prisoners of war, the orders issued by their often-inept, aristocratic officers and commanders played a pivotal role, together with the irresistible human desire for self-obliteration which summarily overrode all other factors. The myth of the resilience and courage of PoWs, largely fabricated in the postwar years when the colonial confidence of Britain was at a low ebb, came to overlayer and obscure the sheer readiness with which the vast military forces sent to protect the British colonies in South-East Asia – often in far greater numbers than their adversaries, as at Singapore in January 1942 – immediately subjugated themselves before the imperial will of Japan and its uncompromised, sexually-ruthless soldiers, who had soon corralled the PoWs into a network of camps around their new territories and were assiduously engaged in initiating them into the far reaches of corporeal bondage. Although Hirohito had ordered that his own forces were prohibited from ever surrendering – and, if cornered, had to stage desperate, all-out charges against their enemies – the PoWs were placed by their captors into a different category within the criminality of surrender. The PoWs were now sexual meat, to be experimented upon at will, or worked to death; they were still human, in the sense that they possessed bodies, but their subjugated status allowed their captors the inalienable right to lacerate and shatter the very core of that human corporeality, with wide-ranging neural and sensory results that oscillated wildly between ordeals of torture and ecstasy. And, at any moment, the prisoners – exempted from all rules surrounding the treatment of PoWs by Japan's refusal to submit its authority to international conventions of warfare – could, without warning, be culled individually or en masse by their new owners. Often, the PoWs were housed in vast wooden dormitories which they had to construct themselves in isolated, malaria-ridden jungle terrains, and were given gruelling work to undertake, such as the intensive building of roads and railways through Japan's new colonies; many thousands of these prisoners soon became skeletal forms, contracting beriberi and acute dysentery, until they swelled-up and expired in great terminal expulsions of liquid excrement and noxious internal fluids. In other locations, where no urgently-pressing forced labour needed to be accomplished, the PoWs could be left to the sexual caprices and experimentation of their guards.

In the punitive regime of the isolated PoW camps, run by guards who would far rather have been rampaging through the cities of South-East Asia and dedicating themselves to fulfilling their Emperor's divine edicts on the imperatives of slaughter-induced conquest, beating was the primary means of subjugation. Prisoners were relentlessly beaten, at regular hours of the day and night, with metal clubs, whips, gun-butts and fists, until the institution of the act of beating had become vitally engrained into their lives, and formed an integral, desired part of their existence. The camps' prisoners, though often at loggerheads with one another about their meagre rations and disputed internal hierarchy, were prohibited from ever striking one another; it was the exclusive preserve of the Japanese guards to inflict and sustain a concentrated regime of beatings which left the young prisoners' backs and buttocks intricately lacerated with a corporeal network of blows and whip-marks, whose striations the guards lovingly inspected and fingered every evening, as the near-naked prisoners, wearing only their excrement-and-semen coated white underpants or hand-made penis-pouches, offered themselves up for obsessional ocular scrutiny by their guards. However, any infraction of the camps' strict code was often punishable by sexual torture to the point of death. One well-established method was the exploding of the testicles. In this torture-strategy, a strip of bamboo, previously soaked in water, was lashed firmly around the recalcitrant PoW's testicles; he was then pinioned-out on the ground with large nails hammered through the palms of his hands, in blinding sunlight and intense heat, causing the knot of bamboo to tighten, gradually squeezing the testicles to bursting point, while the screaming prisoner experienced extremes of sensation, from severe pain to blinding, white-hot orgasm; the bamboo strip would finally strangulate the testicles to the point of extinguishment, causing the scrotal sack to suddenly tear apart under pressure and propelling the unleashed testicles themselves up to twenty feet across the ground or into the air, while the prisoner expired in a searing rush of neural oblivion. On many occasions, the guards would pinion tens of prisoners to the ground simultaneously, and place bets on which scrotal sacs would explode first, and on the likely directions of the flying testicles.

The guards of the most remote camps in the jungles of northern Borneo – with only irregular contact with their commanding officers – also organized their prisoners into compulsory chains of buggery that often stretched for several hundred yards. It was the divine duty of the prisoners, in obeisance to their new owner, Hirohito, to perform their corporeal work with the maximum commitment; the guards meticulously scrutinized the amount of effort being expended by each of the prisoners, who were finally ordered to ejaculate simultaneously, after several hours of frantic action, by a suddenly-expelled shout from the camp commandant. Again, the punishment for any infraction – such as early anal-ejaculation and inadequate or irrhythmic thrusts – was death, with the summary decapitation with a four-foot-long steel sword of the recalcitrant prisoner. A vertical deluge of arterial blood would shoot into the air while the punished prisoner's head would roll away across the mud, and his body, now minus its head, would abruptly break the chain, careering off to one side, its semen still spurting into the air, the legs and buttocks continuing to spasm convulsively for several minutes until the heart-pumped emptying of the body's entire content of blood arrived at the point of cardiac extinction. Another prisoner would then be immediately ordered to take the place of the malfunctioning sexual element, and the chain of buggery would re-establish and sustain its momentum until the caprices of the guards had been thoroughly satisfied. In other regions' camp-systems, the sexual regime of servitude and beatings instituted by the Japanese forces varied widely, though its essential components remained the same. Most of the PoWs soon became fully habituated and attached to their regime of buggery and enslavement, although a scattering of unsubjugated prisoners always attempted to escape into the jungles surrounding the camps, where they were often eaten by marauding, cannibalistic tribesmen who were equally indifferent to the imperial power of both the Japanese and the British, and simply seized the opportunity to try out a new delicacy; very few prisoners escaped their captors.

Once the war had ended and the surviving PoWs had been released – often leaving their camps with great reluctance – the regime of surrender, servitude and sexual enslavement instituted by the Japanese upon their captives was, to a large extent, cast into oblivion. In the British media of the postwar years, the pressing imperative was now that of transforming the memory of the Japanese camps into that of sites of courage and resilience on the part of the prisoners, in order to distract attention away from Britain's pitifully inept and slovenly defence from invasion of its colonies, which – across the world – had begun to demand their independence. As the British Empire shattered, there was an urgent need for emotive, tear-sodden accounts to be told of the indomitable resistance of the PoWs to their cruel masters, and how they had often died in one another's arms from the heartless rigours inflicted upon them by the Japanese. Many of the ex-PoWs themselves even came to accept the veracity of this media construction, and began to retrospectively accord themselves deeply heroic – if entirely passive – roles in the conflict. Although the reinvention of the capitulation and enslavement of the British PoWs failed to avert the wholesale collapse of the British Empire from the late 1940s to the early 1960s, it subsisted as the dominant account of the period. Only a small number of die-hards remained enduringly loyal to the divine values of sexual subjugation that had been instilled in them in Hirohito's camps, and occasionally banded together to reconstruct their chains of buggery in out-of-the-way outdoor locations around Britain; but, without the presence of the lethal element of imminent decapitation that had enlivened the original acts, the reunions eventually ran out of steam. The last gasp of the aged 'band of buggers' came on 26 May 1998, when Hirohito's successor, Akihito, was officially touring Britain and travelled in an imperial procession along The Mall, in the centre of London. A number of ex-PoWs were seen to carefully turn their backs at the exact moment that the Emperor went past. The British media were baffled by this, and even suggested that the act implied some kind of slight towards the genial and suave Akihito, who was primarily concerned with enhancing the reputation of modern Japan and made no sign of even noticing the ex-PoWs' arcane act. However, the Japanese media accurately noted that any group's action of turning their backs and buttocks to the Emperor characteristically indicated an intricate ritual of extreme obeisance of some kind; in the case of the ex-PoWs, who were symbolically inviting the Emperor to bugger them, that act was a reverential but terminal one. Once their final ritual had been completed, the satisfied ex-PoWs dispersed and returned to their retirement bungalows around the coasts of England, Wales and Scotland, in Bexhill-on-Sea, Barry Island and Ayr, to await death, consumed with nostalgia for their days of glory at the service of the divine Hirohito.

However, one strategy of radical subjugation enacted by the Japanese on their prisoners of war which generated little nostalgia was that of crucifixion. Many of the victims and witnesses of the crucifixions of the early 1940s assumed that it was an ironic act of contempt on the part of the Japanese, newly devised for their Christian enemies from the USA and Britain. In fact, crucifixion had been a long-standing means of execution in Japan for many centuries, used on Japanese victims, and was never considered a particularly cruel one, at least when contrasted with techniques of 'slow decapitation' via the use of blunt saws wielded by amateur executioners. Crucifixion (*haritsuke*, as it was known) had simply been a visually spectacular mode of death, intended to demonstrate to a warlord's subjects that the penalty for serious crimes was a painful demise; the agonized victims were finished-off by finally having their tensed bodies penetrated with enormous spears. A number of Portuguese and Dutch Christian missionaries were also crucified after illicitly entering Japan during its centuries of enforced isolation from the rest of the world throughout the Tokugawa era, but those crucifixions were intended as a gesture of politeness towards their victims, who were allotted a Christian mode of death which it was assumed by their hosts that they would surely appreciate. The mass-crucifixion of captured PoWs under Hirohito's imperial regime, however, was not intended as a sign of politeness, and formed part of the gratuitous inflicting of massacre and sexual-violation right across Japan's conquered territory, with the aim of unleashing terror and constructing a vast swathe of cowed, servile populations throughout South-East Asia. The crucifixion of PoWs, especially those from the USA, was also undertaken by Shiro Ishii and his doctors at the Unit 731 death-experiment camp's annex at Anda, but it was used there with the twin scientific aims of maintaining the PoWs in a state of mental alertness and receptivity while they were subjected to Ishii's bacteriological onslaught, and also of simply keeping them firmly fixed to the spot. However, in its more habitual application in PoW camps, crucifixion was utilized purely for purposes of arbitrary cruelty.

On the island of Borneo, one of the places where Japan's imperial mission of subjugation first began to unravel, crucifixion in the PoW camps had become almost a mundane act of spectacle and punishment after the first year of the island's occupation. A mood of lassitude had started to set in among the isolated camps' guards, and they often brought the process of crucifixion to a rapid conclusion, before divesting the prisoner of his flesh and organs. A cook at the Sandakan camp in north-eastern Borneo remembered the crucifixion of a British PoW: 'The prisoner was made to stand with his back to the cross. The Japanese officer stood on the stool with the hammer in his right hand. He then raised the prisoner's left arm and, driving a nail through the palm of the left hand, fixed it to the left arm of the cross which was at the height of the prisoner's shoulders. The screaming prisoner tried to wriggle and struggle, whereupon the guard Hinata held the body of the prisoner against the upright post of the cross and put a piece of cloth into the prisoner's mouth. The Japanese officer then placed the stool towards the prisoner's right and nailed the prisoner's right hand to the cross in the same manner by standing on the stool. He then put the stool aside and nailed both of the feet of the prisoner to a horizontal wooden board on which the prisoner was standing. Then the Japanese officer again stood on the stool and fixed the prisoner's head to the cross by driving a large-sized nail through the prisoner's forehead. The Japanese officer then took a knife and first cut a piece of flesh from the left side of the prisoner's stomach and placed the flesh on a wooden board nearby. He then put a rubber glove on his right hand and pulled out the intestines of the prisoner.' The emptied-out, crucified body was finally left to rot. But the destination of its contents had become all-important for the Japanese PoW-camp guards, and also for the Japanese forces in general, as they found themselves increasingly forgotten in isolated jungle terrains after Hirohito's generals became aware that they had overstretched their resources in occupying such a vast expanse of South-East Asia. The body of the crucified British PoW had provided the essential materials for the abandoned Japanese troops' great obsession: cannibalism.

CANNIBALISM IN THE IMPERIAL ARMY OF JAPAN

During the second half of 1943, the all-powerful Japanese forces that had colonized South-East Asia began to realise that their empire of slaughter was starting to disintegrate. In the Pacific Ocean, the US forces had now initiated their gradual advance, from island to island, in the direction of Japan itself. Japan's control over the supply routes that had brought food and weaponry to the edges of its new empire had been cut to shreds by the US's ascendant supremacy. The troops stationed on the far southern edges of Japan's magnificent empire became uneasy as their supplies suddenly stopped arriving and, after they had been instructed for the last time to fight to the death for the glory of Hirohito, their radios fell silent as their commanders – now preoccupied only with the US advance – abandoned them. The troops had entirely relied on their commanders to instruct them on what they should do, and the divine orders for annihilation had come from their supreme military commander, Hirohito, filtering downwards through the military hierarchy and acquiring greater urgency, until those lethal injunctions finally reached the forces in their isolated jungle terrains. Now, the slowly-starving Japanese troops and PoW guards in Borneo and New Guinea were compelled to instigate a new regime of their own to follow on from that of wholesale carnage and murderous sexual experimentation inflicted on entire populations. After frenziedly consuming the whole of South-East Asia (as though it were the lavish contents of a corporeal department-store), the Japanese forces' new regime was to be that of self-consumption: the killing and eating of one another.

The abandonment of the Japanese forces was total: they were simply ordered by their senior commanders to maintain the territories they occupied, and to defend the imperially-endowed soil with their lives. The Japanese units, comprising thousands of soldiers often aged only seventeen or eighteen, were then left to fend for themselves in some of the most inhospitably hot and disease-saturated areas of the world. Since all food supplies had ended, the Japanese had to search out their own. But while much of the land seized by the Japanese in South-East Asia was rich in fruit and fish, vast swathes of the humid jungles and arid plains of Borneo and New Guinea yielded no food whatsoever. The invading Japanese had already thoroughly decimated the native populations of farmers and turned their lands into fire-blackened, terminated eco-systems. After finishing the last of their ration-supplies, the Japanese began to starve, along with those of their PoW slaves who had escaped being buggered to death; their guns also began to rust in the wet heat and their uniforms became ragged strips of sodden fabric around their emaciated bodies. In many areas, even before starvation became an urgent dilemma, the Japanese had already begun to cannibalize their PoWs, along with some of the inhabitants of the territories they had occupied, for purposes of gratuitous butchery and to inflict pleasurable humiliations on their terrified captives and colonial subjects. But now, cannibalism was no longer a recreational activity: it was a primary obsession.

By the end of 1943, group-cannibalism had become the norm among the Japanese units throughout New Guinea and in northern Borneo; occasionally, fierce attacks by Communist guerrillas and lacklustre assaults by well-fed Australian forces were staged on the Japanese positions, but otherwise they were left alone to pursue their new occupation. Every soldier soon became convinced that nothing could be more delicious than human meat. In different areas, the choice of which soldiers would be killed and eaten varied according to the caprice of the remaining officers – in some encampments, the weakest soldiers faced immediate ingestion, while in others, lots were drawn to determine who would be consumed first. By trial and error, the Japanese soon discovered that almost all of the human body could be eaten, including the anus (often described by survivors as having exactly the same taste and consistency as Osaka squid-rings), but excluding a small number of poisonous bile ducts whose swallowing could lead to their ailing consumer himself providing the next corporeal dinner. The human body comprised a vast network of edible matter. Some of the units in Borneo made contact with the cannibalistic tribespeople of the region (whose isolation and rarefied sense of reality meant that, for them, the current worldwide conflict did not exist except as a set of flickering shadows) for advice; in exchange for several soldiers for their own consumption, the tribespeople provided detailed indications on preserving and roasting human flesh. However, in New Guinea, where the Japanese invaders were detested and even the most remote cannibalistic tribespeople were fanatically loyal to the British monarchy, any approaching Japanese were deemed too disgusting to eat, and were simply slaughtered with total ferocity and hastily buried.

Faced with the lack of co-operation from the indigenous tribespeople of New Guinea, the many thousands of Japanese troops marooned in the jungle-shrouded hills, where nothing edible grew and all wild animals could easily elude the soldiers' inept attempts to capture them, had to evolve their own systematized form of cannibalism. The commanding officers, often former bank employees or 'salary-men' who were themselves only in their late teens and had joined the colonial army in the exhilarated furore of imperial victory two years earlier, organized their units (which were usually around two hundred-strong) into three squads. The first squad seized and decapitated the four or five soldiers chosen for the day's collective meal. The second squad prepared the carcasses for consumption: some soldiers preferred to eat the freshly-slaughtered human flesh raw, and this was simply sliced into chunks, while others preferred it roasted or baked, so fires were painstakingly built in the sodden jungle clearings to cook the still-warm bodies. The third squad's duty was to make sure that no

flesh was wasted – all bones had to be thoroughly gnawed, and special delicacies (such as the eyes and testicles) saved and pickled for consumption on special occasions, such as the Emperor's birthday. Soon, the units had become thoroughly habituated to the routines of cannibalism; since their military duties had entirely lapsed, the intricate rituals of eating one another now expanded to occupy their entire waking lives, and they existed in a permanent state of ravening hunger, impatiently awaiting the communal evening meal of human flesh. The only flaw in their new lives was that the number of soldiers diminished by several more each day, so that by the autumn of 1944, many of the units had consumed themselves down to the last man.

One result of the all-consuming desire for butchered human meat was that sexual acts ceased entirely in the areas controlled by the stranded Japanese units. Their PoW slaves were no longer subject to rigorous regimes of anal rape, the few remaining inhabitants of the villages and towns in the surrounding regions were no longer mass-violated during the troops' search-and-destroy incursions, and even the long-engrained practice of anal intercourse between soldiers – a fundamental aspect of Japanese military life for many centuries – now ceased. The longing for human meat simply obliterated sex, and this engulfing lust was exacerbated by the meagreness of the portions served-up: since there were only four or five roasted soldiers to feed several hundred diners, the troops' obsessional hunger constantly exceeded the amount of flesh available, and they always wanted more. One survivor from a cannibalistic unit remembered: 'We had no sexual appetite. To commit rape would have cost us too much energy, and we never wanted to. All we dreamt about was food. I met some soldiers in the mountains who were carrying baked human arms and legs. It was not guerrillas but our own soldiers who we were frightened of.' Cannibalism had utterly superseded every other preoccupation in the soldiers' fracturing minds. Whenever they now thought of their divine Emperor, he appeared as a juicy slab of blood-oozing meat, freshly roasted and ready to be devoured.

One unfortunate and widespread result of the sustained cannibalism practiced

Opposite: Imminent decapitation of Allied PoW

by the Japanese units stranded in New Guinea was that a collective psychosis developed from their obsession with slaughtered human meat, alongside a more virulent form of insanity engendered by the consumption of too many human brains. All indigenous cannibalistic communities are aware that the systematic ingestion of the human cerebellum eventually spreads viral infections and lethal parasites into the bloodstreams and neural networks of its consumers, and that this occupational hazard of the cannibalistic life-style is best avoided by discarding the brain altogether or through limiting the dangers of its ingestion by only eating it on particular days of the week. The Japanese troops abandoned in New Guinea, however, lacked the expert knowledge of the matter which the region's tribespeople had denied them, and relentlessly consumed the appetizing raw brains of their fellow soldiers with lip-smacking fervour. As a result, their nervous systems began to go haywire, resulting in searing cerebral malfunctions that made them scream with agony and sent them rushing into the jungle to bludgeon themselves into oblivion with their rifle-butts. Together with those two principal causes of the Japanese troops' incipient raving insanity, the ever-present element of maddening terror – resulting from never knowing who would be the next to face decapitation and consumption – contributed to the mass psychosis of the abandoned imperial forces. But even so, the intricate rituals of cannibalism served as a valuable means of promoting group solidarity and cohesion for those troops in their extreme situation.

Once the units had gone totally insane – as their limited supplies of butchered human flesh diminished while their desire to consume it escalated out of all control – they began to conduct hallucinatory experiments into the extremities of the human body. The unlucky soldiers assigned to be culled and eaten were now ripped apart rather than decapitated, and the remaining soldiers would thrust their heads into the half-emptied stomachs and chests of the victims, rolling their faces around among the slithering entrails and attempting to bite out the smaller organs with their teeth, before running madly around the encampments in groups, caked in arterial blood and yelling invocations to the glories of the slaughtered human body. Other troops would attempt to lasso one another with the extracted long intestines, and to insert their fists into the victim's rectum in such a way that their fingers then penetrated through into the eviscerated empty shell of the carcass and could be seen making obscene signals to their fellow troops. Piles of severed heads were collected and could be adopted by the soldiers to carry around, perched on their own heads, attached with strips of cloth. Everything was eaten in the end, before it all began to decay in the sub-tropical humidity. But even in the acute madness of the troops' corporeal experiments, powered by the white-heat of their own parasite-ravaged brains, each military unit's sense of discipline and its hierarchical power structure always remained intact.

Although many abandoned Japanese units in Borneo and New Guinea preserved their contingents of PoW slaves as 'emergency rations' through to the autumn of 1944, almost all of them then decided that the time had come for the PoWs to be finally massacred. Not all were eaten. Despite the increasing starvation experienced by the Japanese troops, which had now reached its terminal phase, they were unwilling to sully the purity of their cannibalistic diet by mixing the consumption of the imperially-sanctioned flesh of their Japanese comrades with that of the PoWs (the 'white pigs', as they were known). As a result, the PoWs were disposed of by being sent under armed guard on lethal death-marches through the jungles, where temperatures soared to forty-five degrees celsius at midday. Other PoWs were dispatched in a final cataclysm of anal rape (despite the distaste for such practices among the Japanese who were now attuned to the obsessional rigours of their diet of human meat), while Hirohito's colonial empire started to implode, and the Australian forces finally began to approach the remote Japanese positions. The PoWs themselves had undergone severe starvation over the preceding year and had often been in raging conflict with one another – brought down to a raw state of virulent meat and bacterial fragmentation – though they were themselves forbidden from killing and eating each each other by their Japanese masters, and had to survive on roots and insects; now, they were gradually exterminated. The last of the exhausted, mentally-shattered Japanese troops were also expiring. When the

Australians finally overran the most isolated Japanese positions in the final months of 1944, they discovered only heaps of slaughtered and emaciated bodies, some partially-eaten, others with their orifices coated in dried semen. The Japanese forces' great experiment of self-consumption had reached its far limit.

In New Guinea, the mortality rate of the Japanese forces amounted to ninety-seven percent, with the remaining three per cent usually in too demolished states of mental health to be able to survive outside lunatic asylums in the postwar decades. Virtually none of their PoW slaves survived. The Japanese units in New Guinea had been ordered by Hirohito's Tokyo-based generals (who had barely looked at the terrain on maps before dispatching over a hundred thousand troops there) to pursue a policy of 'self-sustainability' in the hostile jungle conditions, where they were vulnerable to being captured by skull-shrinking tribesmen as well as being propelled into a regime of starvation and cannibalism by their abandonment. Hirohito's generals responded with outrage to the news that their troops in New Guinea had been practicing cannibalism on one another; the information reached them at a belated stage in the conflict, when the disciplined regime of cannibalism had already mutated into its terminal phase of wholesale obliteration. The cannibalism of Japanese troops by their comrades was formally outlawed by an order from Major General Yukio Aozu, issued on 18 November 1944 (by which time the Japanese units in New Guinea had been virtually wiped-out, and the survivors were too isolated and far-gone even to be aware that such an order now existed). However, Aozu was careful to omit any mention of enemy troops or PoWs: cannibalizing Japan's enemies was seen by Hirohito and his generals as highly desirable and justifiable. In sanctioning the use of cannibalism against Japan's enemies, they were blithely following a grand tradition of utilizing cannibalism as a military strategy, which had existed for many centuries throughout East Asia and China. In subsequent decades, too, cannibalism as a tactical strategy would be revived, as occurred in Cambodia in 1974. While advancing towards the country's capital, Phnom Penh, in May of that year, Pol Pot's Khmer Rouge revolutionary army surrounded the town of Kompong Seila and decided to eliminate its inhabitants by starvation. But the resourceful population of ten thousand people, having already eaten all of the animal life in the town, sent small gangs of fighters each night to seize members of the Khmer Rouge cadres encircling them, cutting their throats and then carrying their bodies back inside the town. On one night, these 'hunting teams' managed to snatch thirty of their young besiegers. The town's inhabitants then ate Pol Pot's revolutionaries, making them into soups and stews, and succeeded in resisting the siege for five months, at which point the Khmer Rouge finally gave up and moved on.

Even in more well-fed regions than Borneo and New Guinea, the practice of cannibalism on the bodies of captured enemy soldiers was rigorously pursued by the Japanese forces. Particular targets for cannibalism were the surviving air-crews of American fighter-planes that had been shot-down over Japanese-held territory, since it had been the loss by Japan of air-supremacy to the USA that had led to the disintegration of Hirohito's glorious empire and made the cities of Japan vulnerable to air-attacks. Hirohito had described Japan's enemies as 'bestial', and – especially when Japanese colonial power was collapsing during the early months of 1945 – it became a celebratory ritual, after the shooting-down of US and British planes, for the Japanese commanding officers to eat portions of the executed air-crews' livers. On 9 March 1945, the commander of the Japanese 308 Infantry Battalion issued an order for the preparation of the flesh of a US 'white pig' for consumption by the battalion officers: 'The battalion wants to eat the flesh of the American aviator, Lieutenant Hall. First Lieutenant Kanamuri will see to the rationing of this flesh. Cadet Sakabe of the Medical Corps will attend the execution and have the liver and gall bladder removed.' During the final stages of the conflict, the fiercely-disputed military battlefields also became the sites of an improvised, fast-food cannibalism. Whenever the US, Australian and British forces became involved in intensive fighting at close quarters with the Japanese and had to temporarily retreat, their wounded or recently-killed comrades would become stranded behind the fighting-line for several hours, before a counter-attack could be staged. The Allied troops would then discover that their wounded comrades had been rapidly cooked and eaten. The internal organs had often been removed, especially the heart and liver, and the captives' heads had been severed, scalped and then boiled. The debris of half-ingested human meat lay scattered on the ground around the gutted and headless bodies. Many of the British witnesses of cannibalism were unprepared for the shattering impact it exerted on their vulnerable sensory capacities, and lapsed into a permanent state of infernal hallucinatory derangement as a result.

The Japanese forces also viewed the populations of their new colonies as readily-available sources of human meat, to be consumed whenever they developed the caprice to add cannibalism to their well-established regime of mass-sexual violation and outright butchery. Even when there were plentiful supplies of other food available, the Japanese troops would nonchalantly slaughter and devour the inhabitants of their territories, whom they dubbed the 'black pigs', to differentiate them from PoWs, the 'white pigs'. In the Japanese subjugation of the Philippines, special attention was given to the preparation of human meat for consumption; the Philippino population became the focus of particular Japanese contempt since they had been the colonial subjects of the USA prior to the arrival of their new masters. During the invasion of Manila, the city's inhabitants had often been taken away to be mutilated, skinned-alive and then cannibalized by the rampaging Japanese forces. Many of the city's young female population were simultaneously sodomized and eaten alive by gangs of soldiers. The Japanese forces stationed in far-flung colonial regions also prioritized the consumption of the tender flesh of their territories' young female population, whenever supply-lines broke down and they began to starve. Then, for once, rape became a subsidiary obsession. A *kempeitai* official, Harumichi Noga, remembered: 'You probably think that many of us raped the local women. But women were not then regarded as objects of sexual desire. They were regarded as the objects of our hunger.' As Hirohito's divine empire progressively fell apart, it became an increasingly urgent imperative for the Japanese soldiers to exhaustively exploit and consume the last remaining colonial inhabitants, to the very last gasp, before they would finally be alone with themselves in their new territories.

By the end of 1944, the Japanese army had entirely starved to death in many of its colonial outposts; in other regions, the emaciated, malaria-wracked troops moved across depopulated, fire-blackened plains where the inhabitants had first been mass-violated and partially massacred on the Japanese forces' arrival, then thoroughly decimated or cannibalized as the abandoned soldiers ran out of supplies. The smoking, silent landscapes of gnawed skeletons passed under the naked feet of the marching Japanese troops – whose boots had rotted to rancid pulp several years earlier – as they trudged backwards and forwards in purposeless but disciplined marches across their blighted territories, from the Philippines to Malaya. Having relentlessly inflicted infinite carnage on the populations of East Asia for over a decade, the Japanese were now heading

towards their own decimation. The forces' commanding officers attempted to maintain a rigid level of obedience and to infuse their soldiers with the sanctity of their imperial mission of death in the oncoming showdown with the US forces. However, a scattering of terminally disabused troops mutinied and headed for the most isolated stretches of jungle, where they lived for decades on fruit and insects, re-emerging from hiding only fifty or more years later, with the hope that Hirohito and his generals would finally have been wiped from the face of the earth.

THE DESTRUCTION OF JAPAN'S CITIES AND THE END OF UNIT 731

Japan was now awaiting its retribution for inflicting its immense onslaught of colonial atrocity and corporeal violation upon East Asia: the US forces were closing in upon its territory from the east and south, while Stalin's Soviet Union was calmly biding its time before unleashing its own invasion from the north and west. Japan's cities were now coming within range of the massive US bombers and the forces of its allies in Europe – Germany and Italy – were also fast-disintegrating. In his imperial palace in the heart of Tokyo, Hirohito frantically demanded that Japan should be defended to the death, and that the entirety of its population – one hundred million-strong – had to be ready to die in all-out hand-to-hand combat with the invading American 'bestial' hordes. Japan would then blast itself apart in vast volcanic cataclysms and vanish below the ocean in a final, divine act of self-obliteration, with Hirohito himself disappearing into the black mouth of sacred Mount Fuji. Meanwhile, the US forces were moving from island to island across the western Pacific, with their huge army of very young troops – most no older than eighteen – staging desperate assaults on heavily-defended coral atolls. The Americans had developed a virulent loathing of the Japanese; since they had no divine leader and no engulfing desire to sacrifice themselves for their country, an all-consuming wrath of hatred instead drove

Opposite: Japanese soldier riddled with bullets

Japanese soldier – suicide by sword

them on. The fighting on the Pacific islands such as Iwo Jima was so dense and murderous that human bodies piled up in great concentrations of lacerated flesh. The Japanese troops – themselves also very young, since the previous generation of soldiers who had enlisted in 1941 were now almost all dead – flung themselves in self-immolating charges at the American lines, often blowing themselves apart with grenades as they reached the US troops. Since it was impossible to bury the hundreds of thousands of dead bodies on the smouldering coral islands, which had no soil, an engulfing stench of death rose up in a near-tangible cloud and swallowed-up the battling troops. The entire conflict became saturated in death, and the young combatants on either side grew utterly obsessed with death and with its imminence for them all, as they fought alongside friends whose heads abruptly detonated into savage storms of pulped cerebral tissue, leaving the intact remainder of their bodies to slowly sink to the ground. Even when the US troops reached larger land-masses and cities,

Japanese soldiers – suicide by rifle

with the US re-taking of Manila in February 1945, death enveloped and overlayered everything, crushing to oblivion the young bodies of both the soldiers and the citizens. The departing Japanese forces slaughtered one hundred thousand Manilans as they prepared to flee, thereby twinning their atrocity-crazed entry into the city of three years earlier with an equally lethal exit, and leaving the city streets inundated with tortured, raped and skinned-alive bodies. In addition, the US commander, General Douglas MacArthur, ordered that much of the city be arbitrarily bombed to a state of flattened obliteration, and a further hundred thousand citizens were blown apart by explosions as their previous colonial masters now replaced their short-lived imperial 'protectors' (although the USA would finally grant the shattered Philippines its independence in the following year).

The US forces finally reached the far periphery of Japan itself on 1 April 1945,

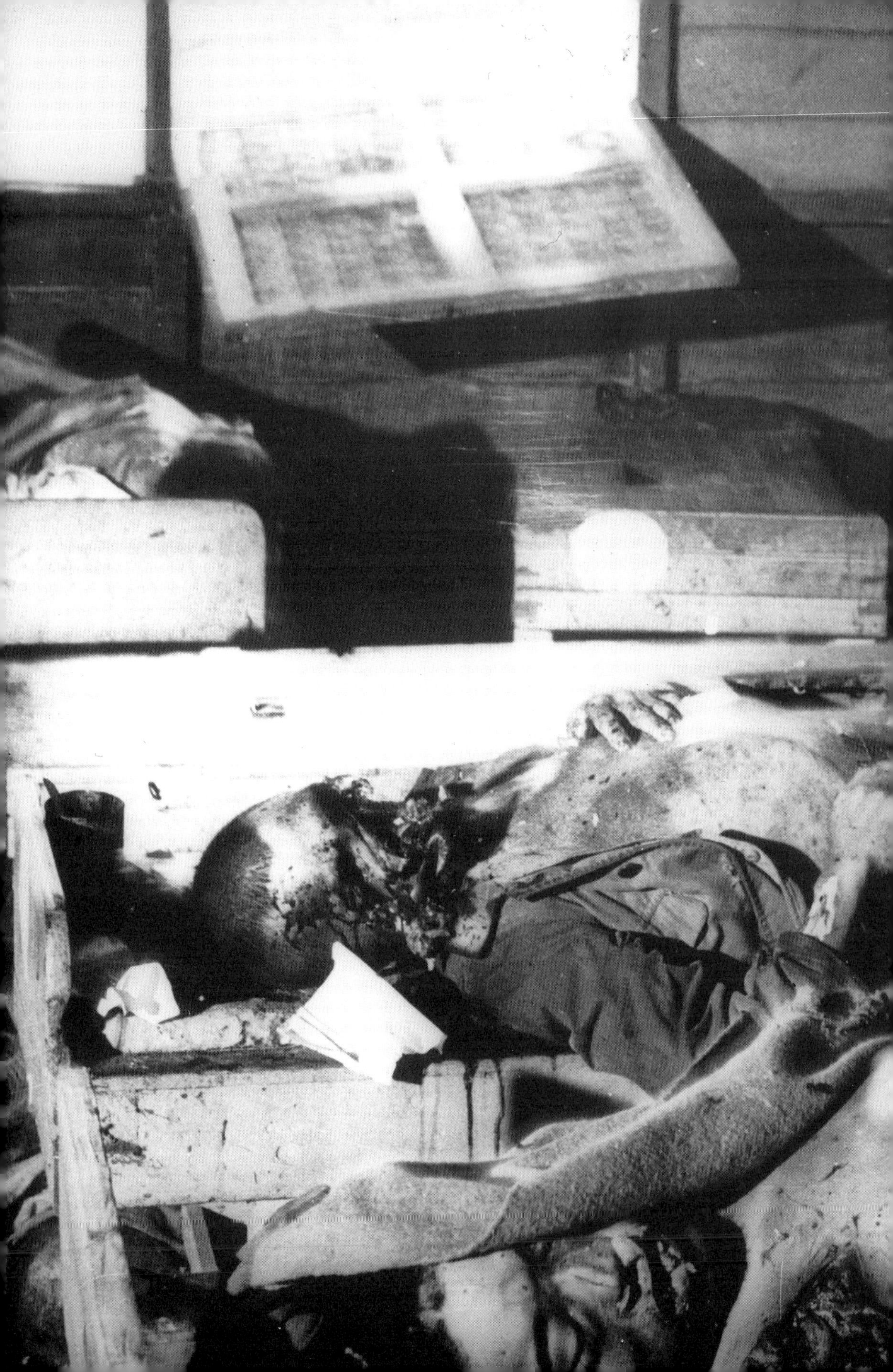

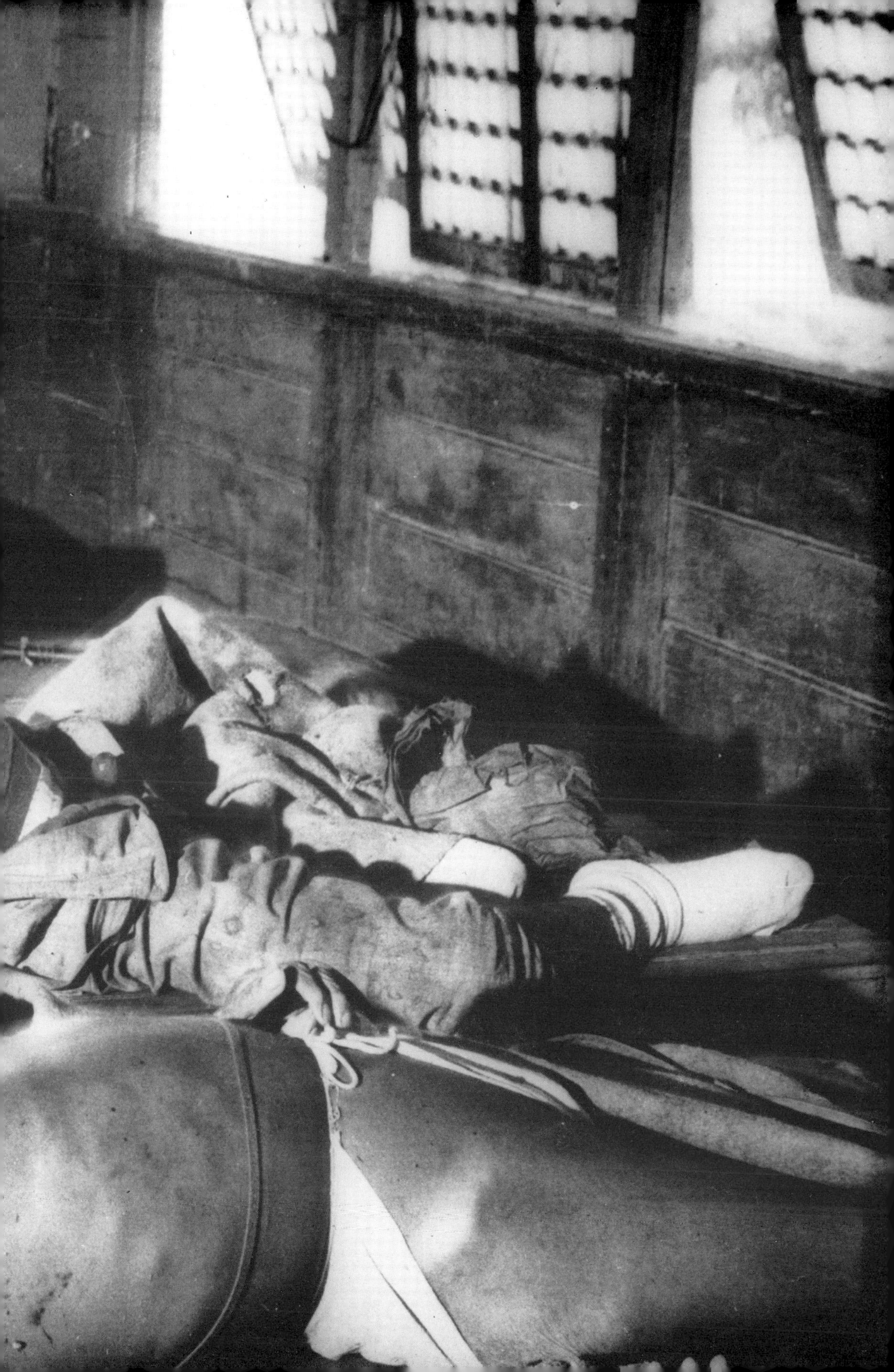

when they landed on the island of Okinawa at the far south-western tip of the Japanese archipelago. The indigenous Okinawans themselves had been colonized by the Japanese in the nineteenth century, and possessed little reverence for Hirohito and his great projects of mass-annihilation. Even so, they were forced by the Japanese military to throw themselves in unarmed charges at the US troops, and to stage vast collective suicides rather than be subjugated by the Americans; the Okinawans' Japanese masters had managed to convince them that the US forces would be even more brutal and murderous than themselves. On other invaded islands, too, many of the female inhabitants had jumped from high cliffs, carrying their children, to be pounded to death on the rocks below, rather than face the wrath of the devilish, rape-obsessed Americans (who, in most cases, wanted nothing more deadly than to hand out tooth-rotting Hershey chocolate-bars). The Japanese troops on Okinawa defended the island in a terminal frenzy, charging the Americans again and again, until they were climbing over fifteen-deep mounds of machine-gunned bodies to reach their enemies. Over a hundred thousand Japanese troops were slaughtered over the three-month period of the battle, while the Americans too sustained heavy casualties. Many of the Japanese built intricate cave-complexes in the island's hinterland, and the only solution for the Americans was to then bring out their huge flamethrowers, which could shoot a long streak of lethal, gasoline-fuelled fire, incinerating anything in its trajectory into smouldering ashes; in the conflagration – accompanied by an ear-splitting cacophony as the gasoline ignited – tens of thousands of Japanese troops had their heads and bodies summarily combusted, usually leaving their legs and feet unscathed. The Japanese who had chosen to hide in caves, awaiting a suitably quiet moment when they could re-emerge in a screaming human-assault of death on the Americans, were instantly melted alive and collectively carbonized into massive assemblages of blackened bone by the flamethrower-inferno. Although surrender had been imperially forbidden by Hirohito, a scattering of Japanese troops, naked and starving, now rushed to prostrate themselves in terror before the American invaders.

On Okinawa, as on most islands they captured on their way to Japan, the US soldiers took no prisoners, shooting any wounded or capitulating Japanese soldiers in the head before extracting the incisors from the butchered corpses' mouths to search for gold-fillings. The Americans had been terminally alienated by the Japanese forces' own treatment of the US troops they had captured in battle, or who had been wounded and then left behind as the Japanese temporarily overran the American positions. When the US troops then recaptured their positions, they would often find that the Japanese had thoroughly tortured their comrades, often slicing off their penises and jamming them into their mouths, then cutting off their arms and legs with machetes and piling-up the severed limbs within sight of the still-living soldiers' eyes, before finally decapitating them. The fighting on Okinawa was marked by the sheer intensity of its corporeal face-to-face confrontations; the soldiers' weapons would often be lost in the mad crush of bodies, and the soldiers would then feverishly throttle one another, gouging out each other's eyes with their fingernails before collapsing in exhaustion. Many of the invading American soldiers had not seen any women for over three years, and were astonished to be faced with contingents of prostitutes advancing towards them in forced suicide-charges. The Japanese army, at Hirohito's instigation, had now instituted a regime of industrial-scale prostitution and rape for its faltering soldiers; hundreds of thousands of the female inhabitants of Japan's colonies, especially Korea, had been arbitrarily rounded-up and sent into the heart of the conflict, where they were then forced into providing seventy to eighty sexual acts each day for the beleaguered Japanese soldiers. On Okinawa, the 'comfort-women' were dragged to the rain-lashed Japanese positions to fellate and be sodomized by the troops even as the massed American forces were rapidly advancing towards the Japanese lines and unleashing their flamethrowers' infernos; tens of thousands of prostitutes were themselves incinerated or blown apart in the mud-sodden chaos of the Japanese positions, while the imperial soldiers desperately rushed to ejaculate their terminal semen into the prostitutes' mouths and anuses at the same moment as they were being abruptly transformed into smoking mounds of ashes and blasted into unrecognizable fragments of scarlet meat.

Out on the ocean surrounding Okinawa, the massed American naval vessels and aircraft-carriers were under aerial threat from Hirohito's secret weapon, the *kamikaze*: these divinely-endowed fighter-pilots had been ordered by Hirohito to sacrifice themselves in glory by crashing their fuel-laden 'Zero' fighter-planes into the inflammable American vessels. The *kamikaze* were known as the 'sons of the Emperor' and the 'hearts of Japan', whose once-only take-offs were marked with collective rituals of the drinking of *sake* rice-wine, distilled from rice which had been symbolically grown by the grateful Hirohito himself in the grounds of his palace; a well-aimed aeroplane, guided by its suicide-pilot, could inflict devastating damage on an American vessel, causing its ammunition stores and fuel reserves to ignite and blowing the ship to pieces. In the six months since the innovation of the *kamikaze* in October 1944, the seven hundred suicide-pilots had caused the deaths of seven thousand American sailors and had sunk or irreparably damaged over seventy vessels. All of the assaults were meticulously filmed by cinematographers in accompanying planes, and the 16mm film-reels were rushed back to Tokyo, to be taken for viewing by Hirohito in the Imperial Palace's cinema (where he also regularly watched the films which Ishii's doctors had compiled of their Unit 731 live-dissection experiments). Around Okinawa, the *kamikaze* now gathered for their final assaults. Not all of them made their attacks voluntarily, or with the sense of divine mission attributed to them in the Japanese media of the time – many were crazed with fear, and simply crashed into the sea at the first opportunity, avoiding the naval vessels. But other pilots successfully hit their targets in sheets of flame and vast explosions of wracked metal and burning oil, instantly cremating both themselves and hundreds of US sailors.

Even before they had finally subjugated Okinawa, the US forces had gained air-supremacy over the cities of Japan. It was now time to destroy those cities and to decimate their civilian populations. On the night of 10 March 1945, a vast air-assault on Tokyo unleashed a city-wide firestorm – a technique also used by the British in their devastation of German cities such as Dresden and Hamburg, in which the dropping of large numbers of incendiary bombs accumulated to create immense waves of fuel-driven flame that rushed through air-less vacuums, alternately carbonizing and suffocating the city's inhabitants. In Tokyo, over one hundred thousand inhabitants were killed in that night; many of them attempted to escape the firestorm by jumping into the Sumida river, whose temperature then rose to boiling point, instantly cooking the tens of thousands of human bodies attempting to keep afloat on its surface. On the following morning, Tokyo's survivors walked through the streets, discovering that their city (which had largely been made of combustible wooden houses) had vanished into thin air. Only a few brick buildings in the financial district had resisted the conflagration. Many hundreds of the city's inhabitants had been suddenly carbonized into still-standing columns of densely-packed ash when they had been caught by the firestorm in the streets; the human columns remained intact until they were touched, then crumbled into tiny cinders and dispersed into the air. Other citizens, lying together on the ground in their thousands as though sleeping, appeared totally unscathed; but they had momentarily breathed a fast-moving wave of fire of extreme temperature, and their lungs had abruptly burned-up and evaporated into steam before being exhaled through their mouths, leaving the rest of their bodies unharmed. The impact of the firestorm had been most concentrated in the poverty-stricken eastern districts of the city, and Hirohito himself survived, along with his palace, located in the very centre of the city.

After the destruction of Tokyo had failed to provoke a Japanese surrender, the US military commanders and the American President, Harry S. Truman (who had replaced the now-dead Roosevelt), decided on a new strategy: the dropping of A-bombs on civilian populations. It was evident that Hirohito and his generals had decided that there was to be no surrender, and that the Emperor's grand plan of having the entire population of Japan ready to tear apart the invading American troops with their bare hands, in a final carnage of total obliteration, was ready to be implemented. On the morning of 6 August 1945, under a blue summer sky, the first A-bomb annihilated the city of Hiroshima: survivors remembered how beautiful the spectacle had been, as the bomb impacted on the city centre, generating an incandescent amalgam of compacted blue, yellow, green, red and white light. Three days later, the second A-bomb was dropped in conditions of poor visibility (the original target, Kokura, had been obscured by cloud, and it was left to the caprice of the pilot to choose a substitute city, Nagasaki, for devastation); the mis-aimed bomb struck the periphery of the city, vaporizing a large part of its population. The entirety of Japan was now a smouldering, terminal zone, with its major cities either firebombed or A-bombed into oblivion (only Kyoto had been spared), and its terrified inhabitants moving chaotically from one end of the surrounded country to the other in their desperate attempts to evade further A-bomb impacts and the imminent invasion of their country by the 'bestial' American hordes. On the very same day as the destruction of Nagasaki, 9 August, Stalin finally decided that it was now his turn to join in with the decimation of the Japanese empire, and he ordered his Siberia-based armies to immediately rampage at maximum speed down through Manchuria and confiscate as much Japanese colonial territory as they could; other Soviet units seized the Kuril chain of islands which extended out north-eastwards from Japan. Within days, Stalin's lethally battle-hardened troops were approaching Unit 731.

Shiro Ishii and his doctors were still working full-tilt on their experiments as the Soviet armies stampeded southwards in vast numbers through Manchuria, raping the already multiply-raped inhabitants and searching out the Japanese colonial troops and their Chinese collaborators to massacre or dispatch to death-camps. Many of the Japanese soldiers committed mass-suicide as Stalin's military death-machine approached: the sheer ferocity of the Communism-propelled Soviet soldiers – who had already thoroughly shattered Hitler's eastern armies earlier in the year and laid waste to the now-suicided dictator's capital-city, Berlin – filled them with terror. Ishii desperately tried to bring his experiments to a successful conclusion, attempting to synthesize a maximum-strength plague-germ that could be unleashed on the Soviet and US forces simultaneously. In his last days at Unit 731, the live-dissections and eviscerations were undertaken at a vertiginous rate, and queues of test-subjects were still awaiting their turn outside the dissection rooms when Ishii finally threw down his scalpel, at six in the evening of 14 August (the day before Japan's capitulation), and, weeping, ordered Unit 731 to be destroyed. Unfortunately, the complex had been built to such high standards, designed to stand for centuries, that it was almost impossible to demolish, even with huge quantities of explosives; the refrigeration block and two of the incineration chimneys were still intact when Ishii's guards and doctors panicked and started to flee. (The abandoned ruins of Unit 731 still stand to this day, now surrounded by concrete-block suburban tenements, built in the mid-1990s for Chinese factory-workers.) Ishii's doctors had been careful to release all of their infected plague-rats and fleas into the surrounding area before they left, unleashing epidemics that would kill thirty thousand of the region's already-decimated inhabitants (Stalin's resilient troops proved to be completely unaffected by the epidemics). All of the remaining prisoners in Unit 731 had been summarily slaughtered without exception, together with most of the heroin-crazed Chinese guards. Ishii himself rushed to the airstrip, carrying the only remaining set of documentation and the films of his experiments (all other evidence was burned), and was flown in his private plane to Tokyo.

All of the senior doctors of Unit 731 also managed to escape back to Japan, on a special train that had been chartered by Ishii, and temporarily went into hiding after they had secretly crossed the Sea of Japan back to their homeland from the eastern coast of Korea. However, almost all of Unit 731's junior doctors and guards were caught by Stalin's armies, as they attempted to flee in panic-stricken disarray. None survived. The Unit 731 guards were simply butchered wherever they were found in Manchuria. After the captured junior doctors had been delivered to the secret police headquarters in the Siberian city of Khabarovsk and subjected to thorough interrogations – often lasting for several years on end, and interspersed with intensive torture sessions, conducted in lethal sub-zero temperatures, that recalled their own Unit 731 experiments into the body's reactions to extreme cold – they were summarily worked to death in Stalin's vast death-camps on the far north-eastern coast of Siberia. The interrogators compiled a report on the Unit 731 doctors' confessions and sent it off to Stalin, who gave it cursory attention; it formed a distraction from his more serious work in the allocation of tractors to Soviet collective farms. However, he ordered that both Hirohito and Shiro Ishii should be arrested in Japan and immediately brought for trial to Moscow, before being sent off to his top-grade Siberian death-camp complex of Magadan. But the US occupiers of Japan refused the request, since they had their own plans for Ishii.

A deal was struck between Ishii and the American occupying authorities in Japan whereby all of the senior doctors who had served at Unit 731 would be given complete immunity from prosecution in exchange for the sole-surviving copy of the documentation of Ishii's experiments, which extended to twelve thousand typed pages. Before long, the anti-Communist US military was having to deal with unrest in its new colony of southern Korea, and Ishii was dispatched (together with several of his senior doctors) in order to undertake a test of his bacteriological knowledge on the 'subversive' elements at work there. On the night of 3 April 1948, a huge uprising broke out on Cheju island, off the south-western tip of the Korean peninsula, where the islanders – appalled at their new subjugation to the Americans, after the colonial Japanese had only just left, and bitterly opposed to their repressive, US-appointed governor, Yu Hae-chin – began the great Cheju Rebellion. Thirty thousand fanatical rebels gathered in the mountainous region in the island's centre and then – simultaneously lighting immense bonfires on all of the mountain peaks as a visual signal to one another – descended in all directions, in a wild frenzy, through the islands' towns, capturing and killing all of the occupying American and Korean troops they could find, together with the island's Korean Christian priests (the islanders had their own, long-standing shamanic and animist religions, and resented the bizarre cult of Christianity which their new colonial masters were belatedly imposing upon them). The priests were crucified, as a gesture of irony, then skinned alive and finally sliced into quarters, before being left in a heap outside the American military headquarters on the island. The US forces were incensed at the rebels' insolence, and – together with the huge Korean militias under their control – used Ishii-inspired bacteriological weapons on the island's rebels, decimating their numbers; the survivors were rounded-up and tortured by the US forces, who then slaughtered the rebels and their entire families by burning them alive and machine-gunning them. Eighty thousand of the islanders were butchered, out of a total population of two hundred thousand; many of the survivors fled the territory of Korea altogether, and relocated to Japan, where they settled in Osaka. The incident comprehensively proved that the US was just as ready to commit colonial massacres and utilize bacteriological warfare as its Japanese predecessors in Korea had been. After years of tension, the Korean War between the Americans and the Communist-led north of the country then began in June 1950, and Ishii was formally employed by the US military, from March 1951, to direct bacteriological operations during the conflict. However, the US's wide-spread but haphazard application of biological weapons on its enemies during the Korean War's battles often backfired, when American soldiers themselves became infected after sudden changes of wind; successful applications of bacteriological warfare required the kind of iron-willed, collective determination displayed by Ishii's select group of doctors during the early 1940s, with their plague-attacks on Chinese cities. After the end of the Korean conflict, only marginally more success was achieved with the hapless use of Ishii's research (after his death) during the USA's military involvement in Vietnam and Cambodia over the next two decades. Finally, in the 1980s, selected elements from Ishii's bacteriological-warfare research were transmitted to the US's then-ally, Saddam Hussein, during Iraq's war with the US's sworn enemy, Iran (which had humiliated and provoked the USA by lengthily holding its Teheran Embassy staff hostage in 1979-81). After Iraq had successfully employed bacteriological warfare in its mid-1980s battles with Iran, resulting in many thousands of deaths, its dictator Saddam Hussein also liberally used it in 1988 to decimate and subjugate the recalcitrant Kurdish population in the northern regions of Iraq, and then went on to disseminate Ishii's work, through a series of lucrative transactions, to go-betweens acting for a wide range of terror-networks, for eventual use on the cities of the USA and western Europe.

In Japan itself, Ishii's Unit 731 doctors were well-treated in the years after 1945.

Many achieved senior roles of responsibility in Japanese industry, while others held positions of power in universities. In 1951, three of the most senior doctors from Unit 731 started Japan's first blood-bank, Midori Juji, using the expertise they had acquired in Manchuria to test blood for bacterial and viral impurities. American casualties in the then-ongoing Korean War were so severe that supplies of blood for transfusion were always urgently needed. Over subsequent years, the business rapidly expanded and evolved into one of Japan's most prominent pharmaceutical corporations. Other ex-Unit 731 doctors also achieved prominent success by exploiting the results and by-products of their research: the scientist Hisato Yoshimura, who directed Ishii's human-refrigeration experiments, went on to become President of the Kyoto Prefectural University of Medicine, where he often lectured on his Unit 731 experiences; accused in the 1980s by the Japanese media of committing criminal acts in Manchuria, he commented: 'Human experimentation? Maybe my subordinates did that, but I never did... Even if that did happen, it was war. The orders came from Japan. The individual is not responsible.' In the postwar decades, regular reunions were held (and continue to be held) of the senior doctors and the few surviving guards of Unit 731, and attempts by the victims of the plague-attacks on Chinese port-cities (nobody survived Unit 731 itself) to sue the Japanese government were always dismissed. Shiro Ishii himself had the least illustrious postwar career of all of the Unit 731 doctors. He worked briefly for his former colleagues in their Midori Juji business, but, unable to reconcile himself to a subordinate position after his years of imperially-invested supreme power at Unit 731, he restricted his activities to serving as a bacteriological consultant to the US military forces and eventually died in 1959; his grave is situated in the suburbs of Tokyo.

Hirohito adroitly salvaged his authority as Emperor, transforming it over subsequent decades into that of a benevolent, patrician figure who had cast the past into oblivion. But in the aftermath of the A-bomb impacts on Hiroshima and Nagasaki, his life itself was in acute danger. After fourteen years of incessantly urging his generals, politicians and military doctors to go all-out for violent imperial expansion – whether or not it led directly to Japan's utter obliteration – he abruptly shifted to a position of dispensing morose wisdom in the days of Japan's collapse. On 14 August 1945, six days after the destruction of Nagasaki, he finally decided on Japan's unconditional capitulation to the 'bestial' US forces. At noon on the following day, his one hundred million subjects – still fully expecting him to berate them to fight to their last breath – listened to the Emperor's stilted, high-pitched voice for the first time, in a radio message pre-recorded on the previous day. Hirohito's statement crackled over the ether, declaring an end to Japan's fourteen-year war and stupefying his subjects with his self-exoneration: 'It was far from our thought to infringe upon the sovereignty of other nations or to embark upon territorial aggrandizement... The situation has developed not necessarily to Japan's advantage...'. Finally, he ordered his subjects to 'cultivate the ways of rectitude'. When the American forces arrived in Japan, it was to a muted welcome, rather than to be torn apart by millions of last-ditch human assaults. The USA and its allies had considered whether Hirohito should be put on trial and executed, but eventually decided that – to prevent Japan from collapsing into total chaos – they would allow him to continue as Emperor, having first renounced his own divinity. The first meeting between Hirohito and the new US commander of Japan, General Douglas MacArthur, took place on 27 September. The affable MacArthur was bemused when Hirohito begged to be killed to atone for the crimes of his generals. At the end of their meeting, at which Hirohito formally agreed to be no longer a living god, MacArthur sent away their interpreters and escorted Hirohito into an anteroom for a private consultation. Immediately afterwards, a single commemorative photograph was taken, in which the minuscule Hirohito, standing rigidly in a formal suit and displaying a slight facial grimace, contrasts sharply with the tall and relaxed MacArthur in his open-necked shirt. Recent digital analysis of the photograph has revealed traces of semen-stains on MacArthur's well-filled trousers and indicates a likely rationale for the new allies' private consultation and the ex-living god's lock-jawed facial appearance. Many of Hirohito's powerful acolytes were far less fortunate; his Prime Minister from the time of Pearl Harbour, Hideki Tojo, was hanged for war crimes in 1948, together with a large number of generals, including Iwane Matsui, who had commanded the army which decimated Nanjing. Hirohito himself survived for another four decades, his reputation retrospectively bleached into innocuousness. He continued to cultivate his benign media-image, while pursuing an interest in the biology of marine-life and regularly planting the imperial harvests of rice, until his death on 7 January 1989.

POST-WAR JAPAN: THE LUST FOR DEATH LIVES ON

With the survival of Hirohito, all of the obsessional dynamics of death and atrocity which had led Japan into creating its divine empire of slaughter and annihilation were transmitted intact into the sensory arena of its postwar cities. During the years of the American occupation of Japan, which extended from General MacArthur's encounter with the ex-god Hirohito in 1945 until 1952, the destroyed Tokyo was shoddily rebuilt, with large areas transformed into intricate warrens of corrugated-iron dancehalls, subterranean sex clubs and experimental art-venues, surrounded by still-smouldering, bomb-levelled wastelands. The imperatives of survival necessitated rampant excess. Large batches of the city's population became corralled into the rebuilding work and spent the rest of their time avoiding the rape-onslaughts of the American troops. But for many of Tokyo's young inhabitants who had escaped incineration in the city's great firestorm of 10 March 1945, that moment of survival had to be seized-upon, and the entirety of the late 1940s passed by in a neural miasma of deviant sexual acts and amphetamine-fuelled alcohol-consumption. The occupying American forces regularly reeled en masse into Tokyo from their bases around the city, such as the immense naval dockyard at Yokosuka, and hurled themselves into marathon, three-week-long sessions of overkill-level whoring, raping and drinking; some of the American occupiers became so thoroughly enmeshed into the extreme sexual furore of Tokyo that they stayed on permanently. That moment of urban bedlam went on until most of the surviving population of Tokyo had been cast into a state of utter sexual subjugation (although the Americans only rarely employed the dual strategy of violation linked to summary massacre that had been pioneered by the Japanese on their glorious East Asia-wide colonial rampage of the previous decade); however, MacArthur then decided that it was time for the Americans to turn their attention to subduing and slaughtering the adjacent Korean population, and testing out Shiro Ishii's bacteriological innovations, in order to protect Korea from the evils of Communism.

Both during and after the American Occupation, Japan settled down into a new regime of murder, with the desire for the arbitrary wielding of death being this time inflicted principally on its own population. Tokyo, above all other Japanese cities, possessed a great lineage of spectacles of death, through its status as the centuries-old venue for state-torture and public executions, and this sustained compulsion to stage and display death would carry itself through into the postwar city. In Tokugawa-era Tokyo, from the seventeenth to nineteenth centuries (when the city had been known as 'Edo'), hundreds of thousands of public executions had been performed before ecstatic crowds, who habitually undertook sex acts or masturbated as the spectacle of massacre unfolded. Executions had habitually taken the form of lengthily-protracted decapitations and mass crucifixions, inflicted on both men and women, often for the most trivial of 'crimes'. Many thousands of the city's inhabitants were gratuitously executed each month, on the sheer caprice of Edo's militaristic governors; their extensive networks of spies reported back even the most minute murmurings of discontent that might conceivably lead to rebellion or dissent on the part of the city's population. At the vast Kotsukappara killing grounds, the recruitment of executioners for the spectacles of death varied according to the social status of the condemned. While aristocrats were expertly and speedily culled by professional executioners, it was a very different matter with the slaughtering of the plebeian hordes: at the start of the execution sessions, a formal request was made to the crowds of elated spectators for amateur volunteers to undertake the killings. It was hard physical work, but there was never a shortage of those eager to come forward and assist. The severest punishment, *nokogiribiki*, involved unhurriedly sawing-off the criminals' heads while their bodies were immobilized up to chest-level in the ground. Specially blunted saws were supplied at the killing-site. Up to three hundred criminals were firmly enclosed in the earth, in long lines, and the sweating executioners went to work in a deranged turmoil of agonized screams, cacophonies of screeching bone, sudden spurts of arterial blood, and orgasmic uproar from the crowd as the heads were finally severed (often after several hours of grunting manual labour on the part of the amateur executioners). The carcasses of the executed citizens were then thrown into a huge pit and covered over with dirt. The site of the Kotsukappara killing grounds and burial pits still survives in contemporary Tokyo, though it was decimated by the city's great earthquake of 1923 (which caused thousands of skeletons to abruptly burst out of the ground), and then ravaged by the US firebombing that whipped through the city in 1945; the diminutive space that now remains from the once-vast killing zone is contained within the grounds of a ferro-concrete temple in a north-eastern peripheral area of Tokyo, Kita-Senju, hemmed in by a contemporary urban landscape of convenience stores and motorway overpasses. With the arrival of the first great wave of European and American visitors to Tokyo, in the final decades of the nineteenth century, the city's system of wholesale public executions abruptly changed. A number of European visitors to the Tokyo region themselves came on the receiving end of murderous assaults, unleashed by gangs of wild ex-*samurai*, from the Satsuma region of southern Japan, who unhesitatingly decapitated the hapless visitors in order to continue the prestigious tradition of butchering Europeans which had begun during the centuries of Japan's isolation from the rest of the world, when Dutch and Portuguese missionaries who had illicitly entered the south of the country were habitually crucified and then hacked into bloody fragments. This long-established custom of slaughtering and then slicing-up European visitors to Tokyo continues to the present day, with incidents such as the July 2000 murder of the English 'bar-hostess' Lucie Blackman, who was drugged, gagged, raped and then suffocated by her Japanese businessman-client, Joji Obara (to whom

The severed heads of executed criminals

she had reportedly promised 'the tongue-lashing of a lifetime' at his seaside apartment in Zushi, on the sea-coast to the south-west of Tokyo), before finding herself being arbitrarily chopped into pieces and deposited in a cave. Towards the end of the nineteenth century, a number of Europeans had witnessed the final public spectacles of human butchery in Tokyo. On 16 October 1873, the correspondent for the London *Times* newspaper reported on a 'vile' mass-execution session: 'I never thought a man's head could come off so easily; it was like chopping cabbages, only accompanied with a peculiar and most horrid sound – that of cutting meat, in fact... There was a dense crowd of Japanese present, including many women and even children; these people never ceased to eat, smoke, fornicate and chatter the whole time, making remarks on the performance, and even occasionally laughing, just as if they were at a theatre.' These public spectacles of execution in Tokyo intimately connected with the often-sexual nature of the crimes committed in the city: murders habitually resulted from sexual frenzies, and owed their detection to furtive observation by neighbours and spies who covertly observed the closely-linked acts of sex and murder while furiously masturbating at the voyeuristically-glimpsed scenes. The European media's disdain for the public performance of decapitation in Tokyo contributed to the adoption of hanging, within prison walls, as the city's principal means of execution from the 1870s, when Japan's long era of military dictatorships had ended and its time-honoured system of divine imperial power was re-instated. The visual spectacle of public mass-carnage sadly vanished and lived on only in the city's collective memory.

By the late 1940s, Tokyo had gained a new and unique layer of horror to add to its already-dense historical strata of atrocity: the human ashes that had become engrained into the city's surface after the mass-carbonizing of one hundred thousand of its inhabitants by the US firestorm-bombing of 10 March 1945. At the same time as Tokyo convulsed in its postwar sexual mayhem, the entire city now also emanated its distinctive aura of death, guiding its conflict-addled citizens into renewed acts of slaughter. One of the first postwar incidents to achieve notoriety in Tokyo was the series of nine rape-killings undertaken in 1945-6 by a veteran of imperial Japan's murderous rampages around China, Yoshio Kodaira, who had been awarded the Order of the Rising Sun (eighth class) for his colonial service, which included the bayoneting of pregnant women and the manual extraction of their foetuses, before eventually being discharged from the military forces. At the end of the war, Kodaira had taken a job as the boilerman at a hostel for female workers, and spent his time assiduously making peepholes in the walls of the women's dormitories in order to voyeuristically watch them undress. He began raping and killing the hostel's residents, and then expanded his activities with a Tokyo-wide reign of rape, often accompanied by lethal strangulation, with his acts remaining largely unnoticed in the chaos of the war's end. Kodaira left the naked bodies of some of his victims in the grounds of the Zojoji temple complex in the Mita district of Tokyo. On finally being caught, after his ninth murder, he was convicted and hanged in October 1947

The legacy of Unit 731 and its bacteriological experimentation on human test-subjects also marked its impact upon Tokyo itself in the postwar years, in a series of deadly mass-poisoning incidents. On 26 January 1948, a well-dressed visitor to the Teikoku bank in the Ikebukoro district of Tokyo announced to the manager that all of the employees had been ordered by the Ministry of Health to drink a liquid solution that he had brought with him, to protect them from an epidemic of dysentery in the district. The bank's sixteen employees each eagerly swallowed two doses of the liquid, before collapsing in agony; twelve of them died. Although a mentally-defective suspect, Sadamichi Hirasawa, was convicted of the murders, he bore no resemblance to the person who had administered the liquid to the bank employees, and his sentence of death was never carried through; over the subsequent decades, it became evident that Hirasawa had agreed to confess to the murders in order to protect a group of ex-Unit 731 scientists who had been determined to assess the virulence of a new variant of their bacteriological experiments on human test-subjects, with the authorization of the US occupying authorities, who had agreed to protect the Unit 731 doctors and planned to further their experiments. However, once the US occupiers had left Japan in 1952, taking Ishii and some of his associates with them to Korea, such incidents abruptly ended in Tokyo. And as soon as the Americans had abandoned their occupation of Japan and left the country, Hirohito immediately seized the opportunity to become a living god again (although he was now a lower-key and less wrathful deity, who remained a constitutional monarch); many of the oblivion-prone inhabitants of Japan were relieved at the re-establishment of Hirohito's muted divinity, forgetting that, in his previous guise, the Emperor had incited them into the headlong campaign of murderous colonial destruction that had backfired into Japan's own A-bombed obliteration in 1945. Other, more disabused imperial subjects were less happy to see the now-genial and reputation-bleached Hirohito return to his habitual position as the object of divine adoration.

By the end of the 1960s, Japan's most celebrated writer, Yukio Mishima, had concocted his own idiosyncratic version of Emperor adoration, with the setting-

Yukio Mishima

up of his private army of young, suavely-uniformed cadres, all of them fanatically devoted in their obeisance to Mishima and in their adherence to the guiding principles of a regime of noble buggery. Mishima had decided to stage a coup in order to demand the restitution of the full authority of Hirohito's divine status and that of the imperial army (which had been limited to anodyne peace-keeping duties by Japan's postwar legal reforms). Mishima had expected his own death to come in the decimation of Japan in 1945, when he had been twenty years old, and he had invested all of his memories of that time of global death with his own sexual compulsions. On 25 November 1970, Mishima held hostage the commander of the military barracks in the Ichigaya district of Tokyo, before appearing on the building's balcony – before a jeering crowd of military cadets and journalists – to incite the inhabitants of Tokyo to rise up in an imperial revolution. He then retreated into the commander's office to commit ritual suicide, slicing his stomach open horizontally, so that his intestines instantly spilled out onto the office carpet. He then ordered one of his cadres his lover, Masakatsu Morita – to slice off his head, but the cadre botched the sword-blow, clumsily butchering Mishima's shoulder instead; another of the cadres had to deputize, whipping off the now-agonized Mishima's head with one adroit stroke. After Morita had also been speedily decapitated, the Tokyo press burst into the office, placing Mishima's severed head (with its expression of horror at its botched decapitation) on the now-sodden carpet in order to take photographs of it. At the same time as Mishima was fatally experimenting with his sexually-inflected imperial preoccupations, Tokyo itself was exploding into riots and violence instigated by the city's anti-Hirohito revolutionary factions, most notably the Sekigun-ha terrorist cell. Before his death, Mishima staged public arguments with the urban revolutionaries, each side locked into its own opposed obsessions and extreme experiments in the elevation or termination of imperial power. The subsequent building of the vast Narita airport, on farm-land close to Tokyo that had been confiscated from peasants, infuriated the protesters, and massive battles erupted in the surrounding area between the police and anarchist revolutionaries, resulting in the deaths of three riot-policemen in a series of ferociously-disciplined human charges and hails of Molotov cocktails. Over the following year, over fifty police stations were attacked and petrol-bombed, particularly in the Shinjuku district of Tokyo, and the lethal intensity of the protests persisted until the mid-1970s. To the present-day, the die-hard remnants of Tokyo's anti-imperial revolutionary factions demand the summary dissolution of Japan's Emperor-system, and threaten renewed terrorism unless the Narita airport is immediately levelled to the ground and its land returned to the peasants.

In the transmission of the dynamics of aberrant carnage from Japan's wartime colonial exploits into the country's contemporary arena, a vital factor has been the random emergence of bizarre, unpredictable cultist groups, determined to unleash an all-engulfing apocalypse on Japan's consumerism-crazed corporate inhabitants. In this new project of obliteration, the ground-breaking work of Unit 731 has proved inspirational, giving religious cultist groups such as the 'AUM Supreme Truth' (with its half-blind and taciturn guru, Shoko Asahara) the ability to launch deadly bacteriological assaults on Tokyo. Most notably, on 20

大島 新大橋
大手町 永代橋

消防庁
東京消防庁
'95 3 2

March 1995, AUM's co-ordinated attack on the city's subway system with sarin gas – part of the massive range of neurally-decimating bacteriological agents pioneered at Unit 731 – proved that the decisive legacy of Japan's wartime experiments is now open to lethal appropriation even by the most peripheral of cultists. The AUM cultists simultaneously unleashed sarin in trains travelling on three Tokyo subway lines that intersect in the district of Kasumigaseki, the centre of Japanese governmental power, at the peak hour of the day when the already-breathless commuters were densely packed, face-to-face, in the overcrowded subway trains. Although Asahara had aimed for massive fatalities, the sarin used was of a deficient quality, and only five people died, with another five thousand temporarily asphyxiated. But alongside the emergence and escalation in prominence of revolutionary and cultist factions, the entirety of Tokyo itself has now become an acutely reactive element in terms of the urban impact it exerts upon the overloaded neural systems of its inhabitants – especially upon its dangerously unstable schoolboy killers – as the city disintegrates into zones of ecstasy and violence.

The lust for obliteration among Japanese teenagers had its first major manifestation outside Tokyo, in 1997, in the provincial city of Kobe, with the decapitation of eleven-year-old Jun Hase and his schoolboy-killer's prominent displaying of the severed head on a school's gate. But even prior to that spectacular event, Japanese schoolchildren had been going haywire at a rapid rate, driven to psychosis in a school system that instituted a regime of infernal pressure, rigidity and overwork, exacerbated by an urban media system that relentlessly provoked shattered sensory responses. By the late 1980s, millions of schoolboys had chosen to entirely isolate themselves in their rooms, absorbed in digital games and fearing their imminent corporeal transformation, within a few years, into that of the despised Japanese salary-men: the anonymous, commuting office-workers who suffer even more hierarchical regimes of subjugation and servitude in their places of work than schoolchildren, finding release only in their lascivious obsession with the rectums and tongues of platform-booted, white-pantied fourteen-year-old schoolgirls. These fears and pressures began to

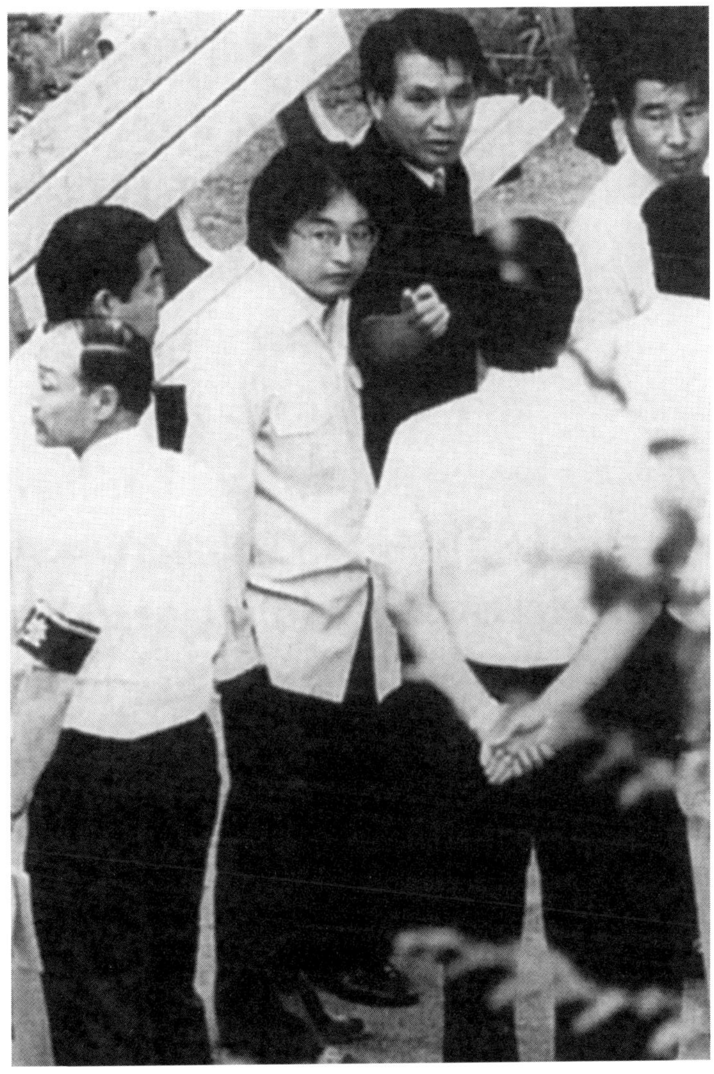

Child-killer Tsutomu Miyazaki (centre)

accumulate into mass-suicides on the part of Japanese schoolboys by the late 1980s, and also articulated themselves in the arbitrary killings, with supreme violence, of schoolboys by their fellow classmates, and in the murders by schoolboys of commuting salary-men, destitute street-dwellers, and small children. A determining figure in the killings undertaken by Japanese schoolboys is the young serial-killer Tsutomu Miyazaki. In 1988, in the far north-western suburbs of Tokyo, Miyazaki began to abduct and slaughter girls of between four and seven years of age; on one occasion, he incinerated the corpse of his victim, then put the ashes in a cardboard box and left it outside the home of the girl's

さあ ゲームの始まりです
愚鈍な警察諸君
ボクを止めてみたまえ
ボクは殺しが愉快でたまらない
人の死が見たくて見たくてしょうがない
汚い野菜共に死の制裁を
積年の大怨に流血の裁きを

SHOOL KILLER 学校殺死の酒鬼薔薇

parents. He always made complete video records of the tortures to which he subjected his victims, and often cannibalized their bodies. On his arrest, Miyazaki disclaimed responsibility and immediately exonerated himself, announcing in court that the 'rat people' had used him as a blameless instrument in the killings of the girls. Miyazaki – whose acts received enormous media coverage – fascinated Japan's schoolboy population with his strange physical appearance and utter lack of remorse. The first comprehensive demonstration that teenage Japan had imploded came five years later, in 1993, with the murder of the thirteen-year-old schoolboy Yuke Kodama by a group of four of his classmates, in a school in the mundane provincial town of Shinjo. Yuke was hunted down to the school gymnasium and then pitilessly culled: his fellow schoolboys attempted to lynch him, then beat him with baseball bats so ferociously that his head turned black and swelled to three times its normal size; finally, he was rolled into a gym mat and suffocated. The murderers instantly forgot their act, and were then astonished to be arrested, although they were to serve only a few months in a detention centre. Schoolboys – and schoolgirls too, in rising numbers – soon realised that it was better to experience the act of killing while still a minor, since they would then go largely unpunished in Japan's legal system; they could experience the sensation of inflicting death without the threat of retribution, in the same way that the atrocity-crazed soldiers of Hirohito's colonial empire could assert that their acts of butchery were divinely-sanctioned and therefore free from all judgement. Both Japanese schoolboys and Hirohito's military forces could expect rapid exoneration after brief, oblivious frenzies of death.

The figure that hovers over the future of Japan – determining its future, and providing it with its seminal, prescient text – is the schoolboy child-killer who signed himself 'Sakakibara Seito' ('Apostle Sake Devil Rose') in a handwritten message which he placed in his retarded victim's mouth before positioning the severed head on the gates of a school in Kobe. His victim had been kidnapped, tortured and then strangled, before being decapitated with a machete. In his message – which generated a media furore in Japan even greater than that focused on the killings of Tsutomu Miyazaki, and whose content closely recalls that of the letters written by Japanese soldiers stationed in 1930s Manchuria to their friends and families at home in Japan – the fourteen-year-old Sakakibara Seito wrote: 'I desperately want to see people die. Nothing makes me more excited than killing. Now the game begins. It's great fun for me to kill people.' The note was signed in English: 'SHOOLL KILLER'. It was delivered at dawn on 27 May 1997. For teenaged Japanese of both sexes, the new game of death – to be played out in their collapsing digital cities, rather than on the subjugated inhabitants of distant colonies – had begun at that moment.

Over the subsequent years, Tokyo itself and Japan's other lacerated cities, such as Hiroshima, became even more deranged entities, traversed at night by escalating teenage gang-warfare and by rampaging *bosozoku* – motorcycle gangs who took their code of rigorous honour from that of the imperially-guided soldiers who had begun their assigned mission of decimating East Asia over seventy years earlier. The motorcycle gangs pursued an uncompromised policy of maintaining the maximum number of violent confrontations with rival gangs, and were determined never to surrender to corporate Japan in the same way that the imperial troops had been instructed by Hirohito never to surrender to their 'bestial' enemies (however, in battles such as Okinawa, the capitulations of naked, starving soldiers had been commonplace – the attempted surrenders almost invariably being met with immediate massacre on the part of the US forces). In contemporary Japan's digital cities of death and ecstasy – in Tokyo, above all – the great seisms of East Asia's murderous twentieth century are now being pulled into a sensory black hole of obliteration, whose future will necessarily sustain and feed the very same vital obsessions that propelled Japan into creating its empire of terminal slaughter – and the future direction of those urban obsessions is entirely subject to the caprices of Tokyo's contemporary young inhabitants.

Part Two

Stalin's Siberia: The Ashes Of The Human Species

STALIN'S EMPIRE: FAMINE, DEATH CAMPS, TERROR

The great empire of Communism subjugated to the will of the Soviet dictator Josef Stalin stretched across over half of the world's landmass. At its maximum expanse, when Stalin had seized control of the countries of eastern Europe at the end of the 1940s, its vast parameters extended from Estonia and East Germany in the north-west, down to Georgia and Armenia in the south-west, and then across endless tracts of frozen Siberian mountains and storm-whipped plains, to Vladivostock in the south-east, and far upwards to Magadan in the extreme north-east. Whereas Hirohito's divine empire of colonial slaughter had been created on the pretext of expanding the constrained territory of the Japanese archipelago, Stalin already possessed an enormous excess of territory. He also had at his personal disposal a massive population, ranging from western Russian intellectuals to isolated eastern Siberian peasants (some of them inhabiting areas so remote and inaccessible that the entirety of Soviet Communism passed by, from 1917 to 1991, without them ever hearing of its existence). Stalin's huge corporeal arsenal was his obsession and the focus of his awesome vision: tens of millions of his subjects would be tortured, frozen and butchered on his caprice, in order to fulfil his grand ambition of annihilating his population for the most arbitrary and gratuitous of whims. In Stalin's Soviet Union, the nature of the human body itself would be transformed by his vision of radical human reduction – by killing the superfluous hordes of his empire in their millions, he would finally concentrate its focus down to a blinding distillation of raw power in one singular and unique corporeal presence: that of his own body, incorporating in its mass of nerves, blood and meat all of the immense glories of Communism. And the pivotal centre of Stalin's all-engulfing project of obliteration would – with the dictator's customary aberrance – be located at the far limits of his empire, in the form of his gigantic complex of death-camps at the outer edge of Siberia, on the perimeter of East Asia: the great extermination zone of Magadan.

The man who would subsequently take on the revolutionary name 'Stalin' (the 'man of steel'), Josef Dzugashvili, was born in the Georgian town of Gori, in the south-western region of the then-Tsarist empire, on 6 December 1878. In Gori, the population habitually lived to be 120 or even 130 years of age, preserved by the mountainous region's pure air, together with the sustained consumption of the area's speciality, Madzhari wine, and large quantities of premium-strength brandy from the adjoining region of Armenia (excessive consumption of Armenian brandy would allow Stalin's future partner in world power, the profoundly-addled Winston Churchill, to live to be over ninety). Stalin was destined from early childhood to be a priest or monk (like his future East-Asian acolyte, Pol Pot) and was sent to undergo many years of religious instruction at the seminary in the town of Tiflis. There, Stalin found a heated atmosphere of feuds and quarrels between the aspirant monks about whether the oppressive Tsar should be overthrown in a violent revolution that would leave the country as a blackened wasteland, or whether the loyal population should remain in their blessed state of absolute servitude. Stalin was soon convinced that a vast onslaught of blood-sodden revolution was the only historical solution for the Russian Empire. In the all-male environment of the seminary, the passionate quarrels between the monks were invariably settled via fierce bouts of buggery, with the strongest monks conclusively winning their arguments by propelling their semen into their opponents' subjugated anuses. Although of short stature, Stalin was sturdy and immensely strong, and he soon became the seminary's pre-eminent tyrant of sodomy, combining his predilection for the writing of lachrymose poetry with his taste for a regime of totalitarian buggery. Stalin left the seminary to become a revolutionary assassin and bank-robber, generating funds for the ascendant Bolshevik terrorist cell, and worked in collaboration with its leader, the bald-pated Vladimir Lenin. Stalin was captured by the Tsar's secret police and sent off to Siberian exile in the isolated penal settlement of Kureyka, where he remained in unsupervised captivity (nobody could escape from Siberia) from 1913 to 1917. Meanwhile, the morose Lenin and his inept band of revolutionaries had taken advantage of the chaos of the First World War to seize control of Russia, dispatching the already-deposed Tsar and his entire family for summary butchery and soon transforming the Tsarist Empire into the still war-ravaged Soviet Union. Stalin arrived back from exile to manoeuvre himself into a position of power alongside Lenin; although the two revolutionaries had ambivalent feelings towards one another (the spluttering intellectual Lenin often derided the uncouth, foul-mouthed Stalin for his stubbornness), Stalin adroitly took supreme power after the apoplectically-inclined Lenin succumbed to agonizing cerebral calcification in January 1924, rapidly elbowing-aside the militaristic fop Leon Trotsky and the sycophantic cliques of Communist intellectuals who had revered Lenin. Until his own death in 1953, Stalin would then wield total power from Moscow, right across the Soviet Union and its massive population, from his office in the Kremlin and his villa at Kuntsevo in the capital's suburbs, generating enormous adoration from his lethally-subjugated but Communism-inspired people. The Yugoslavian writer Milovan Djilas visited Stalin in Moscow on a number of occasions and gave one of the few authentic accounts of the dictator's preoccupations in his book *Conversations With Stalin*: 'An ungainly dwarf of a man passed through gilded and marbled imperial halls, and a path opened before him; radiant, admiring glances followed him, while the ears of courtiers strained to catch his every word. His country was in ruins, exhausted, hungry. He knew that he was one of the cruellest, most despotic figures in human history. But this did not worry him a bit, for he was convinced that he was carrying out the will of history.'

Stalin's idiosyncratic view of history was that it should be totally directed according to his own unpredictable caprices, thereby producing an aberrant momentum that would successfully power the entire Soviet Union and decimate its enemies. That historical vision was to be vitally supplemented by a regime of all-out atrocities and the mass-elimination of swathes of Stalin's own subjects: his top-priority was to urgently reduce the Soviet Union's population by many millions, through gratuitous massacres, in order to intensify and highlight his own pure, corporeally-instilled power. To fulfil this goal, he began to institute a policy of compulsory agricultural collectivization, which led to colossal famines in the 1930s, especially in the Ukraine, and the deaths by starvation of tens of millions of the Soviet Union's inhabitants. The Ukraine became a collective terror-zone in which the emaciated peasants' attempts to take the grain they had grown (which was all arbitrarily confiscated by Stalin's police) were met with summary mass-executions. The people then turned to cannibalism, butchering and consuming their children first, and once they had all eaten one another, entire towns and villages in the region became utterly depopulated. The exhausted inhabitants of other villages, less suited to the rigours of cannibalism, simply starved to death and vanished in great corporeal bouts of terminal screaming. One rare survivor remembered: 'Seeing that death was nearing, the entire village started to howl. In the entire village, peasants were howling – it was not the voice of reason or of the soul, it was like the noise leaves make in the wind, or the rustle of straw. Why were they howling so plaintively? They are no longer human, and yet they cry so. I went out into the fields sometimes and listened: they are howling... And it seems that the whole earth is howling together with the people. There is no God, so who will hear it?' Instead of a god, there was now the atheistic, divinity-detesting Stalin and his totalitarian power of arbitrary human eradication. Once the satisfactory result of the depopulation of the famine-stricken Ukraine and other regions had been achieved, Stalin was able to progress to the next stage in his great work: the capricious re-settling of populations. He ordered all of the inhabitants of particular regions in his empire to immediately leave the homes they had lived in for many centuries, and set off by rail (tightly packed into cattle-trucks, without food, for weeks at a time) for the opposite ends of the Soviet Union; the large Kalmyk ethnic population of the south-west, for example, were summarily dispatched to build new settlements in

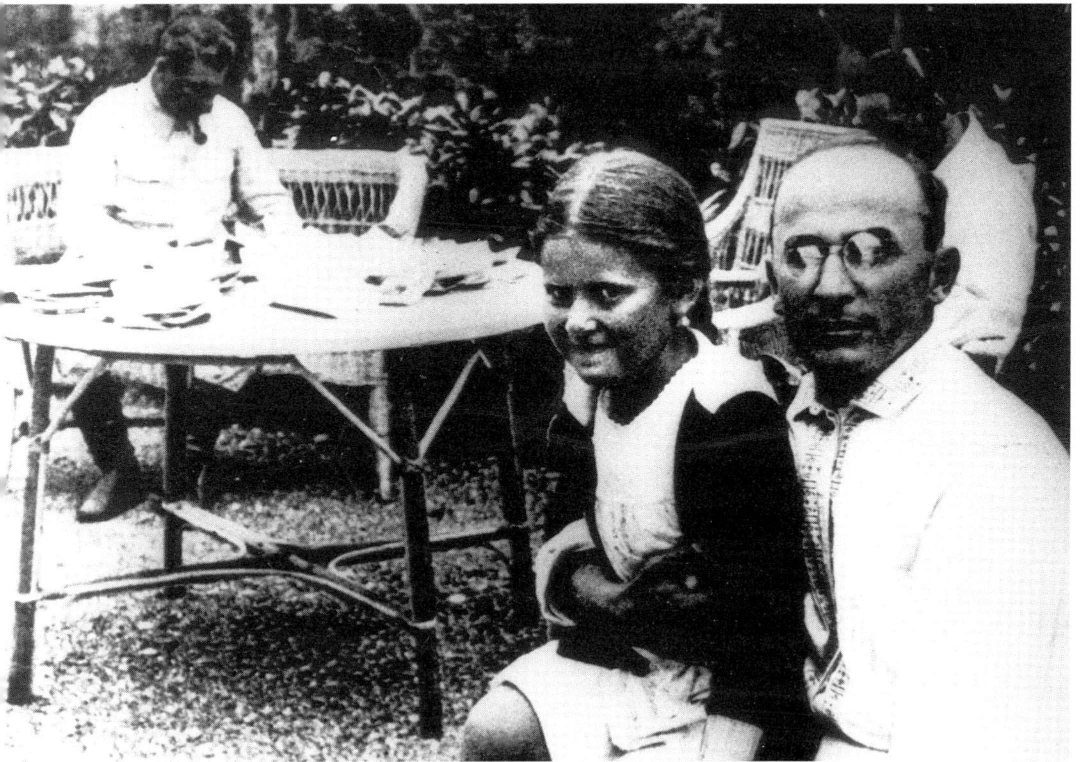

Stalin (left) and Lavrenti Beria (right, holding Stalin's daughter)

north-eastern Siberia. Stalin particularly favoured uprooting populations from the hot regions on the southern fringes of his empire, and re-settling them in the icy extreme north, where temperatures were habitually more than fifty degrees celsius colder than those to which the populations were accustomed; as a result, many more millions of Stalin's subjects were obliterated by being suddenly exposed to acute cold and hunger, and could then be added to his meticulously-compiled human death-toll.

Since Stalin's personal preference was to wield supreme power over the Soviet Union in solitude, he decided in the mid-1930s that the time had come for all of the original Bolshevik leaders to be thoroughly culled. Only one or two servile acolytes, such as the amenable Vyacheslav Molotov (who did much of the practical running of the Soviet Union, working such long hours at his desk that Stalin nicknamed him 'Stone-Arse'), and the cruel thug Lavrenti Beria (appointed by Stalin as head of his vast network of secret police, the NKVD, in

December 1938), would be allowed to survive. Stalin now also decided that millions of his loyal Communist subjects, right across the Soviet Union, were actually 'wreckers', criminally intent on sabotaging his great vision for the country. In turn, the 'wreckers' were necessarily controlled by those in positions of power within the Soviet Union's leadership itself. By extracting confessions from the 'wreckers' through intensive torture (pre-eminently undertaken in the subterranean network of cellars beneath the secret police's headquarters in central Moscow, the Lubyanka), Stalin could then lay the blame for their (non-existent) acts of treachery on his own associates in the Soviet power hierarchy. The torture of the criminal 'wreckers' would often extend over years, until every last fragment of information about their crimes had been collected and sent to Stalin for his leisurely perusal. Some 'wreckers' adamantly refused to confess, insisting that they were loyal adherents to the glories of Communism and fanatical supporters of Stalin's Soviet Union, but they were all eventually ground down with years of cerebral electrocution, beatings of the testicles, and threats to murder their entire families (which were usually carried through). Other 'wreckers' were too eager to please their torturers, and the transcripts of their over-voluble confessions of criminal turpitude exhausted even Stalin. Many of the victims of his first great wave of cullings, in the mid-1930s, were summarily shot in the head in the Lubyanka cellars, while others were publicly tried before the world's media (usually after they had become convinced that their crimes had actually been committed), prior to execution. Stalin's favourite court prosecutor, Andrei Vyshinsky (who adamantly favoured execution without trial), then went to work on his vocal condemnations of the 'wreckers', declaring: 'This is the abyss of degradation! This is the limit, the last boundary of moral and political decay! This is the diabolical infinitude of crime!'. Even the heads of Stalin's own secret police were vulnerable to sudden arrest and execution. Until he gave the job to Beria in 1938, Stalin had repeatedly appointed and then ordered the executions of his police-chiefs – such as the monstrous brutes Nikolai Yehzov and Genrikh Yagoda – together with the other directors and bureaucrats of his regime of terror, with such relentless regularity that he eventually created immense genealogies of the names of those of his murderous acolytes who had themselves been arbitrarily culled and replaced.

Stalin's own personal life was geared to the demands of his duties of all-out obliteration, though he regularly broke off his genocidal obligations to pursue sessions of night-long drinking with his acolytes and henchmen, either in the palatial salons within the Kremlin itself or at his villa in the suburbs of Moscow. In general, Stalin could work for four days and nights without sleep, consumed by the necessity of carrying through his great mission of eradicating large sections of the Soviet Union's population. He had already married twice by the early 1930s, but his wives had a tendency to crack mentally and then expire, from a combination of listening to his interminable diatribes about his counter-revolutionary enemies, together with the effects of his preferred sexual regime of onslaughts of sodomy, which left its recipients with permanently damaged rectums and neural systems. On the night of 8 November 1932, Stalin's second wife, Nadezhda Alliyuleva, shot herself in the head after an argument with her husband; he had been dedicating so much of his time to arbitrary mass-murder and selecting the next part of the Soviet population to decimate – breaking off only to frantically sodomize her while simultaneously railing against 'wreckers' – that she had had enough. From that time, Stalin decided that he would live alone and would require only the sexual services of selected seventeen-year-old devotees to his regime: enormous-breasted 'pioneers' from the isolated regions of south-eastern Siberia, who had fully mastered the shamanic mysteries of sexual ecstasy, and muscular 'super-quota workers' (of either sex) – those who had consistently exceeded the demands of production in Stalin's steel factories, and could effortlessly transfer that Communism-inspired fortitude to output in the sexual arena. Stalin assigned Beria the onerous task of choosing suitably taciturn candidates, ultimately skilled in fellatio, for the weekly sex-parties he now began to organize at his aptly-named Kuntsevo villa.

Through the second half of the 1930s, Stalin escalated his crack-down on his enemies, and managed to remorselessly cull all of the original revolutionary leaders of 1917. His torturers reported to him that the most efficient way to get the once-dignified intellectuals and ex-radicals to confess to their criminal acts was to urinate on their heads. The most important intellectuals, Grigori Zinoviev and Nikolai Bukharin, who had provided the inspiration and theoretical rationale for Lenin's seizure of power, were both tried and then executed (after delays designed to propel them into debilitating states of dread); Bukharin in particular was astonished that his former ally had turned against him, and wrote piteous letters to Stalin, pleading with ever-greater desperation for his life and trying to argue that it was through some terrible misunderstanding that he had been found guilty of plotting counter-revolutionary subversion against Stalin's empire. Until the day assigned for his execution, 15 March 1938, Bukharin continued to beg, in abject terror, for his former colleague in power to pardon him. Stalin adamantly refused to respond, instructing only that the Lubyanka-based executioners of Bukharin and his 'criminal clique' should save Bukharin until last, so that the intellectual would have the leisure to watch the final tortures and executions of his fellow 'wreckers' before his own turn came. Stalin was also finally able to get round to the assassination of the militaristic fop Trotsky, who had briefly struggled with him for power-supremacy over the Soviet Union after Lenin's death, and had now gone into exile in Mexico; Stalin dispatched an adept spy, Ramón Mercader, to summarily cull Trotsky. As well as being a dependable assassin of Stalin's enemies, Mercader was also an expert mountaineer and a skilled wielder of an ice-pick; he was able to infiltrate himself into Trotsky's presence and then viciously drove a specially shortened and sharpened ice-pick deep into the fop's well-developed cerebellum. Mercader remembered that the terminally-lobotomized Trotsky then let out a searing shriek that was 'very long, infinitely long... a cry prolonged and agonized, half-scream, half-sob'.

Only one threat now remained to Stalin's great project of decimating untold millions of his own subjects: Adolf Hitler. The Fascist dictator of Germany had no immediate intention of invading the Soviet Union, preferring to concentrate on rampaging through Poland and western Europe (although he possessed a long-term plan to eventually subjugate the Soviet Union and turn its population into slaves); he regarded Stalin as a proficient dictator, evidently in control of his country with a totalitarian and murderous rigour that – with a little philosophical tinkering – might be worthy of being dubbed 'fascistic'. Stalin, on the other hand, despised the one-testicled Austrian ex-artist with a profound loathing. Although territorial expansion was a low-priority goal for Stalin (he already had far too much), he now had his eye on appropriating the Baltic states – Estonia, Lithuania and Latvia. Beria had reported to him that the six-foot-tall white-blond women of northern Estonia were the most skilled exponents of fellatio in the whole of Europe. On 23 August 1939, Germany and the Soviet Union signed their Non-Aggression Pact, which allowed for Stalin to 'make territorial and political modifications in the Baltic States'. Molotov had deputized for the suspicious Stalin at the signing, although Stalin then dryly sent Hitler his regards, commenting: 'I know how much the German people loves its Führer – I therefore want to drink to his health!'. On 1 September 1939, Germany invaded Poland, and Stalin – unsettled at Hitler's careering assaults across western and central Europe – now decided that he wanted to meet Hitler face-to-face, to discuss the future of Europe. On 19 October 1939, at three in the afternoon, the two dictators met in a sealed railway carriage, in a goods yard outside the city of Lvov (then in the newly-invaded Poland, though now a Ukrainian city). The meeting was a disaster from the first moment. For many years, its unfortunate outcome was kept secret, and only came to light when one of Hitler's surviving valets, Heinz Rösch, was 'interviewed' in March 1979 by the East German 'Stasi' secret police, which had pioneered new standards in torture and was able to extract the long-suppressed information; the original file was then kept in the Stasi headquarters, in the eastern Berlin district of Lichtenberg, until after the fall of the Berlin Wall, when it was stolen and destroyed by neo-fascists, in October 1990. As soon as Stalin and Hitler had come face-to-face, on either side of a map-strewn wooden table, they had begun a ferocious argument about the future division and form of Europe, after the upheavals which Hitler's invasions would necessarily create. The interpreters were unable to keep up with the angry exchange of voices, and the debate soon lapsed into incoherent exclamations from Hitler and expectorated insults from

Stalin, whose temper, when provoked, was brutal. Stalin wanted immediate control of the Baltic States, and – increasingly furious at the sneering Hitler – he abruptly pushed aside the maps which the pair had already scrawled-over with pencil-strokes, announcing that he was going to arbitrarily seize all of eastern Europe, and half of Germany to boot. The heated argument descended into an exchange of blows, and the two dictators' interpreters fled from the room, leaving behind only the petrified valets. Although Hitler was the younger men by over ten years, Stalin's stocky build and long training in the Tiflis seminary soon gave him the upper hand, and he was able to pin the gasping Hitler onto his stomach on the table, and cursorily sodomize him. Within fifteen seconds, it was all over. After glaring at one another for the last time, the two dictators exited from either end of the railway carriage. By the evening, they were both back in their centres of power.

After his inconclusive, misfired encounter with Hitler, Stalin became more determined than ever to take over Estonia and the other Baltic States, with their invaluable resources, and he summarily annexed them in the following year. He assumed that he had now utterly subjugated Hitler, and that he would no longer pose a threat to Stalin's great vision for the Soviet Union's population. But, though he was no stranger to violent buggery, Hitler's angry humiliation increased to boiling point over the next eighteen months, while he was engaged in successfully invading and occupying the entirety of western Europe, apart from Britain, which continued to hold out. In his embittered state of fury, Hitler finally broke off his invasion-plans for Britain and decided instead to divert most of his forces into a colossal, all-out assault on Stalin's Soviet Union, with the intention of leaving nothing behind there but an immense and smouldering black pit in the ground. On 22 June 1941, he launched Operation Barbarossa, unleashing what Stalin would dub the Soviet Union's 'Great Patriotic War'. Although initially surprised at Hitler's tenacity, Stalin was unworried. Although the war would prove to cost the lives of sixty million Soviet citizens and soldiers, the total could simply be added to the death-toll of those of his subjects whom Stalin himself had slaughtered. Like many armies of invasion before them,

Hitler's forces were unable to subdue the vast expanse of Russia, running out of supplies in the freezing winter months at the end of 1941, and suffering enormous casualties before eventually being driven backwards by Stalin's Communism-inspired forces. The result of Hitler's rancorous miscalculation was that Britain was spared an effective German invasion, and survived until the end of the war, while Hitler himself would ultimately become trapped and was forced to commit suicide, in April 1945, in his obliterated capital city, Berlin, surrounded by the now rape-crazed Soviet forces as they successfully completed their lengthy counter-attack; the territory which the Soviet army had seized during its indomitable retaliation against Hitler's botched invasion finally enabled Stalin's empire to gratuitously engulf the countries of eastern Europe, together with half of Germany itself.

In the postwar years, Stalin's struggle with Hitler and his forces' primary role in the total subjugation of German Fascism would occasionally lead him' to contemplate the nature of history itself. He enjoyed obliquely referring to the early period of the Great Patriotic War as that of 'history's lacerated anus'. Stalin was always hazy about the exact meaning of Communism (as his great East-Asian acolyte of the 1970s, Pol Pot, would also be), and never actually read the works of Marx and Engels. However, his comments to an Indian ambassadorial delegation, on 17 February 1953 (his very last day of work in the Kremlin), indicated that Stalin had begun, in his final years, to reflect profoundly on the nature of Communism and Fascism. After the Indian delegation had congratulated him both on his vision of Soviet Communism and on his decimation of Hitler's Fascist hordes during the Great Patriotic War, the nonplussed Stalin quietly commented: 'Communism and Fascism? What are they? They are simply the mouth and the anus of the same whore: Europe... or the whole world. The sole matter of importance is the will and vigour of the man doing the fucking! And to be sure, the orgasm that results from his exertions...'. Although the comments were assumed at the time to be an example of the aged Stalin's crass senility, they subsequently revealed themselves to constitute the great culmination of a philosophical vision of history unique to Stalin, in which

Communism and Fascism had been sexually welded together into a spectacular implosion of the nature of history itself.

However, Stalin's dispute with Hitler and the Great Patriotic War formed only exasperating diversions from his preoccupation with his great project: the large-scale eradication of the Soviet population itself, and the dictatorial enhancement of his own corporeal presence that would necessarily result. By the end of 1936, Stalin's campaign against the criminal 'wreckers' at work in the Soviet Union had reached a critical stage. Since each interrogation and confession of a 'wrecker' led to the denunciation and arrest of thirty or forty more, Stalin soon found himself with a massive surplus of enemies to dispose of. It was now time for him to expand his network of Siberian death-camps, which he had initiated at the beginning of the decade, presciently gauging that there would be the need for vast killing-zones to dispose of many millions of 'wreckers'. In choosing the sites for his death-camps, Stalin nostalgically looked back on his own years of Siberian exile at Kureyka, and chose venues for his camps that evoked the freezing isolation of his own expulsion – the only difference being that very few of the thirty million Soviet citizens expelled to Stalin's death-camps would have the opportunity to make the return journey, as he had. However, the camps able to facilitate a premium-grade level of atrocity would be located even further out than Kureyka had been. For his showcase complex of mass-extermination camps, Stalin had settled on Magadan, in the Kolymskoye Nagor'ye region at the extreme north-eastern perimeter of the Soviet Union, where temperatures habitually fell to minus seventy degrees celsius; camps already existed there, but they would now be massively expanded. Other venues for Stalin's camps were selected in coal-rich areas along the ice-blocked coasts of western Siberia, and also at the northern tip of the Ural Mountains, such as that of Vorkuta, which was much closer to Moscow and could be reached by train in a journey of only several days. However, Magadan – in its East-Asian isolation – would allow for special treatment to be meted out to Stalin's enemies. While the many hundreds of death-camps would enable the frozen boundaries of the Soviet Union to burn with a raw fury of extinguished human lives, the particular attention which

Stalin invested in creating Magadan would demonstrate that it was closest to his heart, forming his own individual annihilation zone. Magadan would be the unique site in which Stalin could carry through his great test-project for the wholesale elimination of the tainted human species.

MAGADAN'S DEATH CITY: THE EXTREMITIES OF ATROCITY

The original idea for the vast East-Asian death-camp complex of Magadan had been formulated by Stalin in the same year, 1931, as his despised enemy, the myopic Hirohito, had issued his divine commands for the murderous overrunning of his new mainland colony, Manchuria, and for the building of the Unit 731 human-experimentation complex. However, it was only from the mid-1930s that Stalin, faced with an enormous glut of 'wreckers' to punish, ordered that Magadan needed to be built up into a colossal city of death that would extend out over many square miles. In his sparse office in the Kremlin, equipped only with a roughly-hewn desk and chair of Georgian cedar-wood and a reading-light whose glow could be seen at night from outside the Kremlin (reassuring the entire Soviet population that their beloved Stalin was always there, toiling on their behalf), Stalin worked immensely-long hours, around the clock, signing the death-warrants of those who were about to be arrested and sent off to his death-camps. Over the twenty-two years from 1931 to 1953, thirty million Soviet citizens would be decimated in the entire death-camp system, with fourteen million of them destined to expire at Magadan itself. On average, Stalin signed over three thousand death-warrants each day, even during the years of the Great Patriotic War; if a particular criminal had already been arrested and had faced torture-interrogations in the Lubyanka cellars, Stalin also needed to scan the resulting confessions, cursing with outrage as he did so. It was a gruelling revolutionary task, but Stalin's only wry complaints to his secretaries about the onerous duties of his great work were that his wrist often became stiff and that the endless days of work had turned his always-seated body into a barrel-shaped mass of meat. Occasionally, he would break off work on signing death-warrants in order to pursue his other main preoccupation: the assigning of tractors to particular collective farms. His only relaxation was the weekly all-out party of terminal dissipation which he staged for his acolytes at his Kuntsevo villa on the edge of the city.

Every night, in each city of the Soviet Union, a train of thirty or more cattle-trucks would be assembled in the railway marshalling-yards, and the 'wreckers' being dispatched to Magadan would arrive in black NKVD vans without windows. Many of them had only been arrested less than an hour before: the hordes of subjugated intellectuals had often been busily writing essays in praise of collectivization and the construction of dams, and the poets had been composing lyrical epics lauding Stalin's vision, when their collective-apartments' doors would be brutally forced off their hinges and a gang of NKVD police would suddenly burst in, truncheoning everybody within range and then arresting the criminals, together with their entire families. The intellectuals' writings would be left unfinished at their desks as – astonished and baffled – they would be driven at speed to the marshalling-yards, and densely crammed in with the other 'wreckers'. The train journey, across the entire expanse of the Soviet Union, to the East-Asian port of Nakhodka, could take up to three months; no food or water were provided, although the prisoners could barter their clothes or the use of their sexual organs in exchange for sawdust-bread and lethal potato-vodka from the isolated, inbred Siberian peasants who gathered around the train whenever it stopped. All urination and defecation had to be done from the opened doors of the cattle-trucks, and the precariously-poised defecators were often left stranded and frozen as the train's jolts sent them flying into icy wastelands in which the nearest settlement was often a thousand miles away. The track itself had been shoddily-constructed in the early 1930s, having been built by the first batches of prisoners assigned for Magadan, the lines laid at furious speed by the prisoners – who froze into solid blocks of flesh, in their tens of thousands, along the route – as the first trains impatiently chugged along behind them. Finally, the cattle-trucks of prisoners arrived at Nakhodka, where those who had survived the train-journey were now dismayed to find that another, much-worse journey awaited them: a four-month-long sea-voyage, northwards up the East-Asian sea-coast for many hundreds of miles, to Magadan. The ships provided by Stalin for the trip were disintegrated hulks of rust with vast cargo-holds, and the prisoners (each ship carried a human cargo of twelve thousand) were simply thrown down into the darkness. On the voyage, the ships' crews and the accompanying NKVD guards killed time by conducting mass-rapes, pulling the statuesque, blond Russian women out of the hold and intensively violating them on the urine-sodden deck, before jettisoning their bodies into the black ocean. Occasionally, the prisoners – driven insane by hunger and their interminable confinement in freezing darkness – attempted to mutiny, screaming insults at the NKVD guards above; the guards always laughed in contempt at the prisoners' futile rebellion and hosed water into the hold until it was full; the water then immediately froze, entombing the entire consignment of prisoners in ice. Every winter, many ships became stuck in dense sheets of ice in the Sea of Okhotsk, after leaving Nakhodka and passing to the west of the northern Japanese island of Hokkaido, then northwards through the Tatarskiy Proliv channel, between the Siberian coast and the island of Sakhalin. The Sea of Okhotsk habitually froze-solid during the extreme winter months, trapping Stalin's ships. The guards and crews managed to survive on their meagre rations and rape-adrenalin until the ice eventually cracked and they could proceed to Magadan, but the howling prisoners in the hold all gradually froze and starved to death.

By the time they reached the dock at Magadan, the surviving prisoners had become *dohodiags* ('those who are coming to the end'). But their adversities were only just beginning. They staggered out of the ship's hold, their ankles and wrists chained together, blinded by the malevolently-grey daylight of Magadan. Above and all around them, a vast cacophony of human screams and an infernal panorama of flame-shrouded mountains, ash-belching chimneys and immense columns of trudging human forms welcomed them to Magadan. None of them knew where they were. The existence of Magadan was known only to Stalin and the NKVD bosses, who were so regularly slaughtered by Stalin that they had no opportunity to make it known (even if they had wanted to); since nobody ever returned from Magadan during Stalin's lifetime, there were no survivors to break its secret. Magadan was a vast city of relentless butchery, populated at any given time by one million enslaved inhabitants, who were incessantly replaced, as they expired, by new citizens from Stalin's great surplus of 'wreckers'; apart from the Magadan dock-area, where the prisoners were given their thin, already multiply-worn black uniforms of rags (many of them were near-naked after bartering-away their urban clothes, months before), there were 170 subcamps and incineration-units, constellated around the palatial complex where the NKVD officers in charge of the smooth-running of Magadan lived. The topography of Magadan was that of a series of recently-created mountains of excavated deep-red earth that rose up from the coast, covered with open-cast mines where the prisoners worked twenty-hour daily shifts, extracting and refining platinum, lead, uranium, silver and other metals. Flames shot up from the prisoners' improvised smelting-works, and the whole of the Magadan complex was suffocated by a great pollution-cloud of noxious fumes that never cleared. For two winter-months each year, the darkness never lifted in Magadan, but the prisoners had to keep working. The quarried metals, including large quantities of gold, were never sent back to Moscow; Stalin was utterly indifferent to wealth, and simply ordered the metals to be thrown into the sea. What interested him was death, in ever-vaster quantities, and reams of documentation on the millions of Magadan's liquidated inhabitants was always thoroughly compiled, bureaucratically-sifted, then flown back to Stalin at regular intervals for his satisfied perusal.

The overwhelming sensory experience of the Magadan prisoners was that of intense cold (habitually minus seventy degrees celsius, with occasional sudden drops into the minus eighties), coupled with the obsession of escaping it. Each day, long before dawn, the prisoners were expelled from the decrepit wooden barracks where they rested for short periods each night, and either sent to work at the adjacent mines, or dispatched outwards on the one road that led northwards from Magadan, to search for new reserves of metals. One of the rare death-camp survivors (released after Stalin's death), Marian Bilewicz, remembered the state of sustained corporeal extremity in which the frozen prisoners found themselves: 'Terrible, inhuman, penalizing labour. In the glare of blazing fires, amid the frozen night, glinted hundreds, thousands of shovels, tossing the snow that was to be swept up by a bulldozer further away from the road. So long as you had enough good sense and strength to remain in motion the entire time, there was a chance of surviving, enduring. But each day, around the fires, a dozen or so huddled human beings gathered, wrapped in every rag they owned. They sat motionless, in a tight circle around the warmth flowing from the crackling wood-chips. They were already living corpses. Nothing could save the health or lives of these people. Warmed from one side by the heat of the fire, grilled by the biting smoke of the burning branches, they were exposed on the other side to the effects of a cold measuring many tens of degrees below freezing. No organism could endure such a gradient of temperature occurring within it. Blood warmed in the veins of the face, hands, chest and stomach was pumped by a weakened heart into a body reduced nearly to a state of hibernation. Something was happening inside the man's body which he could not explain – he was overwhelmed with drowsiness and nausea, overcome by an ever-greater chill. He therefore moved still closer to the fire, crawled practically inside it. After several hours of sitting in this way, there were only corpses by the fire, or men in extreme agony. Nothing could budge these people from the fire. Neither threats of force, beatings, nor attempts to stir the stiffening muscles and cooling blood – nothing helped. After they were pulled away forcibly, they fell like logs into the snow and lay motionless. Not a day passed without a mass of stiffened corpses being carried back to the camp.'

The principal duty of the long series of young NKVD officers whom Stalin personally appointed to run Magadan on his behalf was to create a gratuitous, city-wide state of terror and enslavement, with ever-escalating massacres, rape-frenzies and torture-sessions. Although the East-Asian location of Magadan was far away from the European comforts of Moscow and Leningrad, its

Communism-inspired directors worked assiduously to fulfil all of Stalin's murderous caprices, endlessly circuiting all of the subcamps to inspect their operations and instigate ever-harsher regimes. From their relatively-luxurious villas, positioned in the heart of the murderous cacophony of Magadan, they themselves worked twenty-hour days, devising new means to terminally subjugate and obliterate the population; more and more ship-loads of prisoners kept arriving in an endless stream at the docks, and each of the disorientated prisoners who had survived the journey needed to be immediately assigned to the subcamps. The vodka-fuelled work of Magadan's directors was hard, and only their utter devotion to Stalin sustained them. Their reward from Stalin was to be arbitrarily slaughtered. From the mid-1930s, when Magadan began to operate at full-tilt, Stalin became increasingly exasperated with the inadequacies of his appointees. The first director of Magadan, Edvard Berzin, was called back to Moscow and summarily culled in the Lubyanka for being insufficiently murderous; Berzin was then replaced by Stiepan Garanin, who was culled for being a 'Japanese spy' (although the uneducated Garanin pleaded to his torturers that he had never even heard of Japan); Garanin was then replaced by Andrei Vyshnyevtsky, who was culled for being insufficiently murderous; Vyshnyevtsky was then replaced by Ivan Nikishov, who was culled for no reason at all, just after Stalin had slyly decorated him with the 'Order of the Hero of the Soviet Union'; the rapid succession of directors went on and on, throughout the twenty-two years of Magadan's operation.

The most infamously carnage-obsessed director of Magadan was Stiepan Garanin, who was in his mid-twenties; although of peasant origin and possessing limited intelligence, the suavely-dressed Garanin's arrogance and sense of mission were total. His devotion to Stalin was all-consuming. One of the few prisoners to survive Magadan, Anatoly Zygulin, witnessed Garanin at work on his round of camp inspections: 'I saw Garanin from close up, just like I'm seeing you now. He was reviewing a column of prisoners. And he wasn't alone, but with an entourage. Before he appeared, they were relaying messages over the telephone: he might pull up here, so as to personally conduct an inspection of the camp. He was still in Magadan when we were already standing at attention. Everything cleaned, painted, the ground strewn with yellow sand. The camp guards fret and fume; they cannot control their nerves. Suddenly, whispers: They're coming, they're coming. The gate of the camp opens wide. And he drives through it with his escort – several passenger cars, several trucks carrying his personal guards. He steps out of the first car, and his entourage arranges itself quick as lightning on both sides. All of them with Mauser pistols, in short sheepskin jackets. He himself in a coat of bear fur. A fierce expression on his face. Drunken eyes, heavy as lead. The commandant of our camp, a major, rushes up to him and reports in a trembling voice: "Comrade director! The independent subcamp 78 of the Magadan camp system ready for inspection." Garanin barks: "Are there prisoners here who shirk their work?". "There are," the major answers fearfully. And around twelve people step forward from the ranks. "So, you don't want to work, you motherfuckers?". And he already has a pistol in his hand. Bang! Bang! Bang! He gets them all. Any that still move are finished off by the entourage. "And are there record-setters here, those that exceed the quota? Super-quota workers?". "There are, comrade NKVD-chief!". A joyful, cheerful line of super-quota workers steps forward. They don't have anything to fear. Garanin walks up to them with his entourage, still holding the Mauser with the empty magazine. Without turning around, he hands it backwards to his people. He gets from them a new loaded pistol, which he puts into a wooden holster, but he doesn't take his hand off the butt. "So: super-quota workers? You exceed the quota?". "Yes!" they answer. And he asks them again: "Enemies of the people who exceed the quotas?... Hmm... you, cursed enemies of the people! One must liquidate the likes of you...". And again: Bang! Bang! Bang! And again around ten people are lying in a pool of blood. Then he appears cheered up, his eyes have grown calmer. He has sated himself with blood. The camp commandant leads his dear, honourable guests to the banqueting hall for a prepared feast. And he is happy that he has himself dodged the bullets. When Garanin felt like it, he shot the commandants of the subcamps as well. It was a terrible lawlessness, when Garanin was chief. People fell like flies.'

The entire regime of the Magadan complex was rigorously run on principles of arbitrary slaughter and capricious cruelty, in order to conform absolutely with Stalin's preferred strategy for the decimation of the Soviet population. This strategy presented Garanin and his fellow directors with the twin compulsions of butchering as many of the death-city's inhabitants as possible, in the shortest possible time, while also imparting a vitally feral, uncompromised element to their acts of mass-slaughter. Nothing at Magadan could be predictable or mundane – but, at the same time, millions of criminals had to be systematically exterminated. As a result of these dilemmas, the Magadan guards and subcamp commandants existed in states of petrified tension as lethal as those of the prisoners themselves, knowing that they could themselves be instantly butchered if they appeared to be conducting their duties too routinely. The optimum moment for them to abruptly cudgel to death the prisoners was at the open-air roll-calls which marked the beginning and end of the day of work, and ample scope also existed for prisoners slaving-away in the open-cast mines to be suddenly singled-out and offhandedly culled by their overseers. Prisoners could be clubbed into blood-sodden oblivion both if they committed any infractions to camp discipline, and if they did not: they were equally, terminally guilty – Stalin himself had already signed their death-warrants. In that freezing landscape of shattered bodies and screams of terror, they would never know the exact moment of their deaths, and lived on in a state of temporary suspension of execution (provided by their benevolent patron, Stalin) until the due moment would come for the prisoners to be all gratuitously eliminated.

The subcamp commandants and guards operated a slave market on the quayside at Magadan, and had the right to choose any of the reeling, dumbfounded prisoners emerging from the death-ships, to act as their sex-slaves. Whenever the Magadan directors made their bi-yearly visits to Moscow to receive Stalin's commands (although almost none of them would actually survive for a period of two whole years), Stalin ordered quotas to be set on the number of sex-slaves to be owned by the guards – seven at any one time – and also insisted on a scrupulous regime of anal penetration, grumbling irascibly to the Magadan directors that he was in the business of decimating the Soviet population, not allowing it to increase. Although they had been comprehensively starved, abused and mass-raped on their journeys to Magadan, many of the sturdy young Russian women were resilient, especially those (during the final years of Magadan) who had already served in the Great Patriotic War, when shock-troop units of entirely-female soldiers rampaged across the German lines, during the hand-to-hand battles to re-take Byelorussia, in order to ferociously ambush the astonished young Fascists and excise their penises as souvenirs. Some of the young women were able to convince themselves that their obliterating journey to Magadan held a higher purpose, and that their intensive mining-duties and sex-servicing of the often-moronic subcamp guards valuably demonstrated their indestructible commitment to Communism and to their glorious leader, Stalin. At the slave market, the guards' sexual preferences varied according to their Soviet home-region: those from Armenia and Georgia seized-upon the white-blond, pneumatically-breasted women from the Baltic States, while those from the northern Soviet Union habitually selected the swarthy, vicious-tempered women from the hot regions of Turkmenistan and lower Mongolia.

Since temperatures at Magadan were often so dangerously sub-zero that any exposed flesh would immediately congeal into ice, and any unleashed fluids would freeze and permanently adhere-together the sexual organs of two copulating human bodies, it was imperative for all sex-acts to be urgently-conducted, in blurred frenzies of sodomy. Even so, it was often the case that a guard and his sexual victim (whether a slave, prisoner, or another guard) would be sealed-together in a frozen medium of solidified semen, extending between penis and anus, whenever the guard's blast of neural ecstasy made him neglect to limit the sex-act to less than four seconds. In such cases, it was necessary to send for Garanin, who would immediately blast-apart the cerebellums of the lethally-fastened pair with his Mauser, adding yet another instantaneous burst of white-hot sensory incandescence to the guard's now-destroyed brain. Although some guards would keep their sex-slaves in operation for several weeks, or would barter them with other guards, all were summarily butchered in the end. The brutal, near-cretinous guards particularly enjoyed culling the female urban-intellectuals and poetesses at Magadan, whom they contemptuously named the 'little flowers' and subjected to collective bouts of double and triple anal-penetration, before they abruptly cudgelled their howling victims into the void. The habitual brevity of sex-acts at Magadan was also the result of the long hours of work undertaken by the prisoners – of the four hours when they were not toiling at the open-cast mines, two hours were spent in trudging from their barracks to the mines and back, and another two were used-up in attending the rigorous roll-calls that marked the beginning and end of the working day. As a result, all sex-acts, eating of meagre rations, sleep and open-air defecation had to be concertinaed into less than ten minutes each day. And as the years of Magadan's operation went on, Stalin progressively cut the amounts of rations received by both guards and prisoners, until all sexual activity finally ground down to nothing, in a listless, hallucinatory state of terminal starvation.

Once the prisoners at Magadan had cast off the mortified bewilderment which they all experienced on arriving at their destination, they responded to the lethal environment of the death-city in different ways. Many simply dropped dead in terror. Others – former Moscow bureaucrats, party-members, and previously-coddled members of the urban intelligentsia – soon succumbed to the regime of vicious beatings from the guards, supplemented by relentless starvation and exposure to cold. But others were able to adapt themselves to that regime, and once they had understood that it was unlikely that they would ever leave their new East-Asian home, accustomed themselves to life at Magadan. Some of the prisoners even tried to institute their own intricate power-systems and regimes of torture, violence and subjugation to inflict upon one another, chopping off each other's fingers, stealing one another's threadbare uniforms, and putting out each other's eyes with needles. But, whenever the guards caught sight of such strategies, they immediately crushed the skulls of the perpetrators with their metal clubs – Stalin alone (and they themselves, as his representatives) held the absolute monopoly over the infliction of murderous servitude. In the dilapidated barracks which housed the subcamps' workforces, the prisoners occasionally had several minutes to rest on the dirt floors, clustering-together to lessen the effects of the biting winds which whipped through the flimsy planks of the buildings. Then, they spoke to one another about Stalin. The camp regime outlawed all verbal communication of any kind during the twenty working hours each day, although howling and screaming were permitted. After several years of captivity, most of the prisoners had forgotten almost all of the Russian language, and – pressed tightly together in their barracks – could recall only one word: 'Stalin'. All conversations consisted of that name, grunted, expectorated, whispered and murmured, in a one-word language that articulated the entire experience of Magadan and of the Soviet Union itself.

As the 1950s began and Magadan reached the twentieth anniversary of its inauguration, the camp's death-toll had far exceeded the ten-million mark. The bodies of many prisoners had been incinerated in furnaces, whose chimneys disgorged the corpses' ashes upwards into the sky, but they soon fell to the earth again, and gradually accumulated into heaps, then into hills, and finally into black mountains of coagulated human ashes, alongside the red-earth mountains that had resulted from the years of mining excavations. Millions more bodies were thrown into pits which often took the prisoners months at a time to dig, in the frozen earth: the ice-preserved bodies stubbornly refused to decay, and the millions of corpses continually returned to the earth's surface, their facial expressions at the moment of death intact, whenever the winter's movements of ice scoured away the bodies' covering of earth. The extreme landscape of Magadan – with its sub-zero temperatures, ice-storms and darkness – exacerbated the regime of death imposed by Stalin upon its inhabitants, maintaining and compulsively displaying that regime's lethal traces. By the beginning of 1953, Magadan had evolved into a terminal city of annihilation that possessed a time and space of its own. The only time that existed was that of slaughter and oblivion, and the only space was that of the Magadan death-city itself: the existence of the rest of the world had been utterly forgotten. The presence of Stalin himself began to fade away. All of Magadan's surviving inhabitants – both the prisoners and the guards – were now starving on decreased rations, and endlessly hallucinated in a frozen stupor of fear and obliteration. Even during the Great Patriotic War, the death-ships had never stopped arriving from Nakhodka, often bringing mystified prisoners who had gone directly from repelling the Fascist hordes to being dispatched by Stalin to Magadan. The end of the Great Patriotic War in 1945, with the crushing of Hitler and the Soviet invasion of Manchuria, far to the south of the death-camp, had been a negligible event at Magadan: nothing changed, and the ship-loads of criminal 'wreckers' kept arriving. The barracks gradually deteriorated and blew away in the winter storms, and the prisoners were compelled, during their rare moments of rest, to lay huddled-together on the frozen earth, in the open air, beneath the blasts of fire and the never-dispersing shrouds of poisonous fumes expelled by the crumbling smelting-works. Magadan still screamed, in its vast over-accumulation of death.

THE DEATH OF STALIN

At the end of his life, the body of Stalin had come to form the supreme pinnacle of the Soviet Union's revolutionary grandeur, incorporating within itself all of the heroic elimination of the Soviet population in the death-camp city of Magadan, and at the many other extermination-camps across Stalin's Empire, together with the slaughter of vast quantities of 'wreckers' in the Lubyanka torture-cellars, and the decimation of millions of recalcitrant peasants in Stalin's great famines and arbitrary transfers of populations. Stalin was now universally known by his utterly-subjugated subjects as 'The Boss'. He could do anything he wanted to them. His corporeal glory was evidenced in the all-engulfing cult of Stalin, with every Soviet city carrying thousands of his portraits on immense, illuminated hoardings along its streets, and every home bearing photographs of his glowering face on its walls. But despite the absolute pre-eminence of Stalin's corporeal triumph, constructed over decades through the arbitrary culling of tens of millions of his subjects, that body had now started to fall apart. On his visits to Stalin, the Yugoslavian writer Milovan Djilas noticed that he had acquired the 'Kremlin complexion' of those who sat for decades on end at their desks: the blanched face, with intensely red cheeks, topping a sack-shaped body of concertinaed raw meat. Djilas commented: 'His teeth were black and irregular, turned inward. Not even his moustache was thick and firm. Still, the head was not a bad one; it had something of the common people, the peasants, the father of a great family about it – with those yellow eyes and a mixture of sternness and mischief.' Although Stalin's body was crumbling, he still fully expected to live on into the twenty-first century (as many people of his generation from Georgia would indeed manage to do), fuelled by a diet of Madzhari wine, triple-strength Armenian brandy and premium-grade fellatio. He continued to issue orders to vastly extend his network of death-camps further and further, to the extremes of the Soviet Union and then beyond, worldwide; then he would top off his brilliant career in annihilation by exacting the wholesale eradication of the human species.

By the first months of 1953, the ailing Stalin was spending most of his time at his Kuntsevo villa in the Moscow suburbs, surrounded by his bodyguards, his Georgian cook and his valet, Ivan Khrustalev. He had discovered that he could sign even more death-warrants by cutting out the thirty minutes of daily commuting between Kuntsevo and the Kremlin, in a speeding black Zil limousine: the culling of another nine hundred criminal 'wreckers' each day could be facilitated by his remaining at his desk in Kuntsevo. Every week, he organized a night-long debauchery-party at which senior members of his leadership would be required to drink heavily and then systematically humiliate themselves. As well as sex-acts, the evenings also included film-shows, usually of pornographic films involving collectivized peasants in traditional costumes and farm animals; Stalin was a self-appointed film expert, and insisted on viewing every single film made in his domain, in order to decide which should be shown in cinemas and 'palaces of culture' right across the Soviet Union, and which should be arbitrarily censored and burned (their directors often disappearing forever into the Lubyanka cellars). The cruel Lavrenti Beria was a permanent fixture at Stalin's parties; like Stalin, he was a death-crazed, brutal Georgian, and had decided that the time had now come for Stalin himself to be culled. The ambitious but spindly-framed Beria was ready to take over the top job, in order to escalate the slaughter-frenzy initiated by Stalin; for him, Stalin's great crime was that of being 'insufficiently murderous' – the very same misdemeanour with which Stalin himself had charged many of his ill-fated Magadan directors. Along with Beria, Stalin's weekly guests also included the survival-obsessed sycophant Molotov, and a new, ascendant addition to the Soviet leadership, the genial and beerbarrel-shaped Nikita Khrushchev, from the Ukraine.

On the night of 28 February 1953, the invitees to Stalin's Kuntsevo sex-party included the usual trio of Molotov, the cruel Beria, and the shaven-pated Khrushchev, together with a white-blonde, six-foot-tall, seventeen-year-old Estonian super-quota worker, Inna Merilo. Stalin, having annexed Estonia in 1940 at Beria's urging, in order to analyse for himself the astonishing fellatio-skills of its white-blonde, six-foot-tall, seventeen-year-old women, was now making full use of the region's resources (Estonia, subjugated to the rigours of Communism for over fifty years, would only be released from the power-grip of the Soviet Union at its collapse in 1991). Inna Merilo, who had consistently exceeded quotas in the steel-factory to which she had been assigned, thereby attracting the attention of the NKVD, remembered: 'Everyone knew what the devil Beria wanted our loyal super-quota workers for. We heard that he "tested" Estonian candidates for Stalin's parties by having them cocksuck him, while he held one of those dreadful instruments for the slaughtering of cattle to their heads, shooting the bolt into their brains as he ejaculated, unless he was sure that they would meet Stalin's standards. The motherfucker! As a result, I was forced to hone my skills to an ultimate level of expertise. I had no choice – I wanted to survive.' At the intensive sex-party on the night of 28 February, held in a private salon at the rear of the Kuntsevo villa, Molotov was made to dance to the point of exhaustion in a cocktail dress, while Stalin relentlessly consumed eleven bottles of Madzhari wine; then, the devastatingly-beautiful and naked Merilo, with her seven-inch tongue, rapidly began to propel the grunting Stalin, still dressed in a grey military uniform with only the fly-buttons undone, towards a fellatio-generated, brain-destroying neural apocalypse. Simultaneously, the drunken Khrushchev decided that he would assert his ascendant power over the unprepared Beria, and abruptly engaged him in a headlong struggle of buggery, which Khrushchev (three times the weight of Beria) easily won, pinioning Beria down on the red-silk carpet and sodomizing the howling totalitarian with a precision-aimed series of devastating, alcohol-fuelled anal thrusts. Meanwhile, Stalin himself was being adroitly fellated to the point of orgasmic sensory wipeout; his brain's blood vessels lethally split apart with a sound that could be heard in the room, as a series of detonating whip-cracks. The entirety of the Soviet Union and the glorious power of Communism had become concentrated down into Stalin's fast-imploding corporeal presence and his collapse into terminal incapacitation.

For the whole of the next day, Stalin lay – purple-faced and groaning – in a pool of urine and semen on the salon floor. Beria, despite his humiliation at the hands of Khrushchev, had successfully carried through his grand plan, while Khrushchev had been so drunk that the entire evening was consigned to addled oblivion in his aching head, and both Molotov and Inna Merilo had simply fled in terror. Stalin's valet, Ivan Khrustalev, was in the pay of Beria (who had promised him the directorship of Magadan), and kept the Kuntsevo bodyguards from entering the locked private salon until the late evening, by which time Stalin's decimated cerebellum had congealed into a mass of black pulp. Finally, his bodyguards burst into the room and found Stalin close to death. Even so, his determination to stay alive, and take more of the incandescent oral punishment which had been meted out to him, kept Stalin stubbornly breathing for a further four days. Beria remained kneeling by his side, looking inconsolably at the expiring dictator, whose power of speech had been reduced to the repeated expulsion of one vicious expletive. Stalin's team of terrified doctors applied leeches to his body, and took x-rays of his shattered cerebral network. On the evening of 5 March, Stalin began to writhe in a series of spasmodic corporeal

Dead Stalin

contortions, then began a terrible death-agony of blood-congested choking; finally, he directed a last mad glare at everyone in the room, raised his fist, and died.

A moment later, Beria rose from his knees in exultant triumph, barking: 'Khrustalev, my car!'. He immediately left Kuntsevo and set off for the Kremlin in order to occupy Stalin's sparsely-furnished office, signing death-warrants at full-tilt and attempting to take over exactly where 'The Boss' had left off. Vast queues gathered outside the Kremlin to view the dead body of Stalin, which was cosmetically enhanced to erase the traces of the sensory frenzy which had provoked his premature demise. All of the eastern European Communist leaders stood beside Stalin's carcass to ostentatiously weep for the benefit of the newsreel-cameras which were recording the scene. Then, the grief-stricken population of Moscow began a psychotic stampede of death outside the Kremlin, as a final tribute to their butchery-crazed leader, with over two thousand people being summarily crushed underfoot and fatally pulped. The entire population and immense landscape of the Soviet Union then fell silent and still for several days, astounded at its survival. The body of Stalin was gutted, chemically preserved and then placed alongside that of Lenin in his vast, darkened mausoleum, where millions filed past the spotlit ex-tyrant, cautiously making absolutely certain that he was dead (since Stalin's corpse tenaciously continued to grow stubble for several days after his demise, this remained in doubt). Stalin himself had not wanted to be placed alongside Lenin, where it appeared that he was in a position of subordination to the bald-pated intellectual, and he had demanded that – should he die – he had to be buried in the eleventh-century Gelati Monastery in western Georgia, which he had visited in the year before his demise and which would then become known as the 'Monastery of the Immortal Stalin'. However, even his place in Lenin's mausoleum was short-lived. On 31 October 1961, a squad of young Kremlin guards was dispatched to Lenin's mausoleum to dislodge the corpse of the healthy-looking Stalin, who still appeared as though he were alive. The contemptuous guards dug a hole in an insignificant location beside the Kremlin's wall, threw in Stalin's body (after ripping off the gold buttons from its military uniform), collectively urinated on its well-preserved face, and then hurriedly covered it over with dirt.

Although Beria had seized absolute power over the Soviet Union on Stalin's death, his regime was to be short-lived. Khrushchev soon teamed-up with the equally barrel-sized Georgi Zhukov – the general who had ferociously obliterated Hitler's forces in 1945 and had precipitated the hapless Führer's suicide as Zhukov's troops had rampaged their way towards his bunker in Berlin – and they then decided to give the upstart Beria his come-uppance. On 26 June 1953, three months after Stalin's death, they invited Beria to a gathering in one of the meeting-halls at the Kremlin, at which they would give him their total allegiance. The unsuspecting Beria sat at the top of the table, and was suddenly surrounded from behind by Zhukov and six of his equally-burly generals. Khrushchev then yelled: 'Get up! You're under arrest!'. Zhukov lifted the spindly-framed, white-faced Beria out of his seat, wrenched his arms upwards behind his back, and bodily carried him out of the room. Beria was then wrapped up in a carpet, thrown onto the floor of a Zil limousine, and driven at high-speed to the Lubyanka, where he was dispatched to an isolation-cell. After Beria had been left in total solitude for a period of six months, in an ever-increasing state of terror, never knowing when the moment of his execution would arrive, Zhukov and two of his officers abruptly burst into his cell on the night of 23 December 1953; they blindfolded the screaming would-be dictator and dragged him into another room, in which a foot-long curved spike protruded from the wall. His hands were tied behind his back and then his body was hauled off the ground and slammed backwards against the wall, so that the hook penetrated deeply into his anus, causing him to wail in agony. One of Zhukov's officers then placed the barrel of a Mauser pistol to his forehead, while Beria desperately tried to win a few more seconds of life, yelling: 'Permit me to...'. Zhukov yelled to the other officer: 'Gag the bastard with a towel!'. One of Beria's eyes glared in wild horror at his executioners over the top of the blindfold, which had been sent askew by the force of his impact with the wall. The officer then pulled the trigger, and the top of Beria's head disintegrated into a scarlet mist of brain tissue and skull fragments. Beria's assistant in the demise of Stalin, the treacherous valet Ivan Khrustalev, was culled on the same day.

Although Khrushchev, who then took power, was an all-out, fist-pumping dictator with a tyrannical style of his own, he was never demented with the all-consuming desire for inflicting mass-death and terror in the way that his now-moribund Georgian colleagues, Stalin and Beria, had been, preferring instead to spend his time taunting the USA with his fast-growing arsenal of A-bombs, and strengthening the Soviet Union's hold of subjugation over its eastern European 'satellite' states, especially Hungary. As soon as he had consolidated himself in power, Khrushchev ordered that all of the death-camps which Stalin had so painstakingly constructed, over a period of twenty years, were to be immediately shut-down, including the death-city of Magadan. All of the criminal 'wreckers' and death-camp prisoners were instantaneously given full pardons and ordered to be liberated: they were now free to return to their homes. He also indulgently dispatched the lethal super-quota worker Inna Merilo back to her native-city of Tallinn, instructing her to keep quiet about whatever had happened at Kuntsevo (which he himself had, in any case, been too obliterated by alcohol to remember) and assigning her to a job as an usherette at the recently-opened Stalinist 'palace of culture' in Tallinn, the Sõprus. Then, Khrushchev began his work of denouncing Stalin to the entire world and propelling the Soviet Union off on another, less-murderous tangent towards the moment of its eventual extinction, thirty-eight years later.

Many thousands of miles away, on the East Asian coast, the survivors of Magadan heard the news of Stalin's death and of their own liberation only after a long delay. Magadan then had nobody in command – Stalin had only recently culled the latest in the long line of inadequate, butchered NKVD directors, and had not yet found a suitable replacement at the time of his death. As a result, there was no-one at Magadan with the power to issue the official order for the prisoners' release, and the camp's regime went on as usual for nearly a year, in its now-hallucinatory state of starvation, slaughter and searing cold. The death-ships stopped arriving, and the camp's population rapidly diminished without its fresh supplies of criminal 'wreckers'. Finally, Khrushchev sent a new director, who stayed in the storm-lashed, poisonous death-city of darkness for the entire five minutes it took him to issue the order to close down Magadan with immediate effect, then resigned and jumped back into his plane to return to Moscow. By that time, it was March 1954, a year after Stalin's death, and only three hundred thousand prisoners remained alive, along with eighty thousand guards; they were all abandoned, including the subcamp commandants and guards, and left to make their own way back to their original European home-cities, such as Moscow, Leningrad and Stalingrad. Everyone – the subjugated and the torturers – had now been placed on exactly the same zero-level. Although a few guards were summarily bludgeoned to death by irate prisoners, most of the population were too far-gone to experience anger, or even to react to Stalin's death. Gradually, they abandoned Magadan; the city's twenty-year-long shroud of pollution fumes lifted, and the blasts of smelting-fire and columns of incinerated human ashes abruptly ceased. Without maintenance, all of the shoddy camp-buildings rapidly fell into ruins in the extreme East Asian climate. For some of the population, it was a deep wrench to leave behind the landscape of terminal carnage, with its familiar mountains of human ashes. Some of the more resilient prisoners had survived for years on end at Magadan (a handful had even been there for the entire period, from 1931 to 1954), and lingered in the ruins of the buildings for several more years; the last prisoners departed in 1959. One particular problem was that it was nearly impossible to leave Magadan. There were no ships, and the last plane to use the haphazardly-tarmaced airstrip had been the one carrying Khrushchev's director. The only road was that leading northwards, into oblivion. As a result, it often took the prisoners a decade or more of walking, through the icy terrain of Siberia, to reach their homes. Most perished while attempting to cross the impassibly sheer Verkhoyanskiy Khrebet mountain range, five hundred miles to the west of Magadan; the few who eventually managed to reach the eastern Siberian city of Yakutsk then only had an infinite wilderness left to cross. Some of the remaining survivors headed south for several years, through vast, snow-covered mountain ranges where human beings had never been seen before, finally reaching the trans-Siberian railway at Dzhalinda; then, having no money to buy tickets, they simply followed the track westwards towards Europe. No more than two hundred survived the journey; the last arrived back in Moscow in 1971. Even then, they discovered that they formed an alien species in urban Russia, now full of sullen, long-haired teenagers, mini-skirted shopgirls and polyester-suited bureaucrats. The Magadan returnees wandered uncomprehendingly through the cities, often finally succumbing to the long-delayed, obliterating effects of Magadan and falling dead in the streets. The few who survived were the living ghosts of atrocity.

The traces of Magadan have now almost vanished. Even the vast, blood-red mountains that accumulated from the decades of open-cast mining excavations have been gradually eroded down into indistinct masses by the endless storms whipping in westwards from the frozen Sea of Okhotsk, and by the ice-encrusted winds blasting eastwards from the wastelands of outer Siberia. The black mountains formed from the congealed human ashes of millions of butchered bodies, built up over decades from the incineration chimneys' deposits, have also almost entirely disappeared, scoured by the glaciated covering of ice that presses down on the surface of Magadan during its winter-months of absolute darkness. All of the barracks and NKVD villas that constellated the site of the death-city have been utterly erased, leaving behind only scattered strands of barbed wire, cartridges from revolver bullets, and rusted bludgeoning instruments. But, beneath the surface of Magadan, the densely-layered bodies of millions of its slaughtered inhabitants remain intact. The subterranea below Magadan is maintained at such intensively sub-zero temperatures, the earth constantly replaced by never-melting substrata of compacted ice-deposits, that all of the six or seven million bodies of those victims of Stalin who were thrown into vast pits after their killings became enduringly preserved by the intense cold. (An equal number of millions were transformed into human ashes.) The facial expressions of the victims at the moment of death – mass-violated, beaten, shot out-of-hand, or simply frozen – remained vividly conserved, as corporeal memories of genocide. But, with the effects of global warming, Magadan is now thawing: in the years to come, the once-impenetrable plug of ice that refrigerated those millions of bodies will crack open, and finally be blasted off by the sheer physical and gaseous pressure of the millions of expanding, finally-decaying corpses. The resulting corporeal explosion into the open-air, carrying an equivalent impact to that of an A-bomb, will detonate across the northern extremes of East Asia, marking the final expectorated malediction – launched against the tainted human species – of Josef Stalin.

Although the mountains of incinerated human ashes which he bequeathed to East Asia's evidence of atrocity have now largely vanished, Stalin remains a vital presence for both Europe and East Asia. In the western Russian cities, vast demonstrations are staged on the anniversaries of Stalin's birth and death, and many of the countries that resulted from the fragmentation of the Soviet Union's collapse – from Kazakhstan in the south to Byelorussia in the north – are controlled by regimes loyal to the tenets of Stalin, equipped with torture cells and killing-zones at their cities' edges for the disposal of dissidents and enemies; although such regimes are often screened by a tenuous layer of 'corporate democracy', their abiding inspiration is the memory of Stalin, which remains deeply infused into the contemporary forms of Europe. Throughout the former Soviet Union, in the face of state-led, saturation-level corruption, a resurgence of adoration for Stalin has created a tidal-wave of nostalgia for his determined wielding of power, and for his comprehensive acts of slaughter (which are exonerated as occasionally overzealous strikes against enemies, during a period when the very existence of Russia itself was under threat from Hitler). In contemporary Russia, innumerable schoolchildren still revere Stalin, with the accompanying desire that he should now resuscitate himself, in contemporary Europe, and begin his work all over again. But it was in East Asia, in the late 1970s, that Stalin's great projects were most effectively reactivated, and adapted for use in the attempted elimination, via systematic extermination and sexual subjugation, of an entire population – in Pol Pot's Cambodia. But Stalin's aberrant uniqueness, as a perpetrator of mass-carnage, could never be replicated.

Part Three
Pol Pot's Cambodia: Terminal Zero Zone

POL POT: ANNIHILATION ZONES

The Cambodian mass-murderer and revolutionary leader Pol Pot inflicted a vicious and permanent scar of burning atrocity on the final decades of the twentieth century in East Asia, and the seisms of that action point the way forward towards the next century of East Asian carnage. Pol Pot himself conceived of the most ambitious project ever realized to exact a vast sensory holocaust on the people of his own country and beyond, displaying a unique will to obliterate humanity which is unparalleled among the twentieth century's great figures of carnage. At the end of his four years of power, Pol Pot left behind a stunning legacy – Cambodia, on its liberation from Pot's reign of terror, comprised zones of immense killing fields of steaming human meat, with towering pyramids of human skulls stacked up around its cities. A quarter of Cambodia's population had been exterminated, the victims often having suffered months of torture before being summarily clubbed into oblivion. After Pot's departure, the remainder of the traumatized population wandered at random around the country for years on end in the rags of the black pyjamas which Pot had instituted as the national uniform of his people. Pol Pot had marked the brutalized face of East Asia forever with his vision of pure atrocity.

The mysteries surrounding the acts of Pol Pot have only been elucidated in the years following his sex-induced death in the isolated jungles on the Thai/Cambodia frontier in 1998, nearly twenty years after his fall from power.

Only now is it possible to answer the question of how a genial prince from the lower echelons of the Cambodian aristocracy came to order the obliteration of three million of his fellow countrypeople – and how his vision of a national state of absolute murderous power allied to supreme sexual experimentation came finally to be perverted and overthrown, leaving him vulnerable to falling victim himself to arbitrary lusts for death and domination. Pot himself left journals of personal fragments and revolutionary polemics which answer these questions, along with the testimony of survivors and the evidence of atrocity that is enshrined in Pot's own bizarre conflation of Unit 731 and Magadan, in the form of Tuol Sleng, the former colonial school building also known as Death Facility S-21, where untold thousands of Pot's enemies, allies and innocent victims alike all met their ends before having their perforated skulls and shattered bones scattered across fields of watery mud.

Pol Pot was born on 12 January 1925 in the rundown provincial palace of Kompong Thom, ninety miles to the north of the Cambodian capital, Phnom Penh; his real name was Saloth Sar and he took the revolutionary alias of 'Pol Pot' (akin to Josef Dzhugashvili's alias of 'Stalin') only when he began his revolutionary work at the beginning of the 1950s. Pot's family had the reputation of providing the most exquisitely beautiful and sexually-adept courtesans to the Cambodian royalty, and his four elder sisters all trained intensively in mastering the techniques – particularly that of inflicting 'blinding ecstasy' on their sexual partners – which had been developed in the Cambodian aristocracy for over eight hundred years, since the period of the twelfth-century Angkor Empire which had extended out across South-East Asia from the immense temple complex of Angkor Wat, close to Kompong Thom. The greatest of all the Angkor emperors, the leprosy-ridden despot Jayavarman VII, had combined the running of an empire of vast wealth and cruelty with the desire to achieve ultimate sexual self-obliteration before his leprous body fell entirely to pieces, and Pol Pot spent his childhood listening to the legends surrounding the great tyrant, who had lived to the age of ninety, ruling his vast empire with an iron fist (at least when it was not deeply embedded in the supple anal receptacles of his courtesans), while his scribes compiled vast anthologies of intricate sexual positions and his architects transposed these to the many thousands of statues that decorated the Angkor Wat imperial temple complex, which at that time stretched out for eighty square miles. It was only natural that Pot's sisters would use their adolescent younger brother to test out their rigorous sexual experiments, since it was expected that by the age of fourteen they would be dispatched to the imperial palace, now situated in Phnom Penh, and to have achieved complete mastery of the 'eleven great secrets of sexual obliteration' before they began to service the then-ruler of Cambodia, King Sisowath Monivong. Pot's favourite sister, the sexually adroit and lethally beautiful Saroeun, rose to become one of the dissolute Sisowath's most preferred courtesans, and contributed to his death by neural exhaustion in 1941, but she would not survive the arbitrary mass killings of her brother's regime thirty-five years later.

At the time of Pot's childhood, Cambodia was a 'protectorate' of the colonial French government, which had usurped power in the country at the turn of the century in order to exploit the mainly-agricultural Cambodia's gem wealth. Innumerable French playboys and intellectuals passed through the 'exotic' Cambodia of the 1930s, passing on venereal disease and the latest fashions in European philosophy in equal measure to Cambodia's own gullible intelligentsia and aristocracy, which at that period remained in utter awe of French colonial and cultural power. However, a few young Cambodian aristocrats were starting to resent their arrogant French masters, whose sole purpose in visiting or living in Cambodia was to commit the maximum number of acts of anal intercourse with beautiful young Cambodians of both sexes and to steal the surviving statues from the Angkor Wat temple complex for transportation to French chateaux, as well as to systematically plunder the country's gem resources, leaving the vast majority of the Cambodian population in complete poverty. As he grew up, Pot began to view the colonial French in a caustic light. At the age of fourteen, at the moment of the outbreak of the Second World War in Europe, he was sent to Phnom Penh to train as a monk (it was traditional in his family for the male children to devote their lives to the austere demands of religion, to 'atone' for the sexual excess of their courtesan sisters) and was able to view the supercilious French expatriates from up close, particularly since he himself was as beautiful as any of his sisters and had to fend off the constant attentions of the buggery-preoccupied French colonials. He also watched with distaste over the wartime years as the spineless colonial French capitulated in rapid succession to the Germans and the Japanese, and then set up a servile regime in subjugation to the glorious Empire of Hirohito.

At the close of the Second World War, with the defeat by the American and British forces of the Japanese in South-East Asia, the disgraced but tenacious French nimbly managed to re-establish a provisional hold on Cambodia and finally put in power a successor to Sisowath, the equally-dissolute lavish spender, Prince Norodom Sihanouk. One of the manifestations of France's attempt to maintain its grip on colonial power was to grant scholarships to young Cambodian aristocrats such as Pot to spend three years in Paris, with the aim that they would receptively absorb French culture and then return to their country as fervent supporters of continued French domination of Cambodia. (However, over the years that Pot was to spend in France, its colonial hold on Cambodia gradually diminished – largely as a result of the humiliating military defeats which the French suffered against the anti-colonial army in its neighbouring 'protectorate' of Vietnam – and by the time Pot returned to his homeland, France was finally ready to release the country from its grip and allow it to become nominally independent.) In the summer of 1949, Pot confronted the dilemma of whether he should desert his homeland for France, but, faced with the choice of pursuing a monk's severe life of relentless self-flagellation in a Buddhist monastery in Phnom Penh or the adventure of leaving for Paris, he eventually took the latter option and sailed for Marseilles, then took the train for Paris, arriving in the French capital on 20 September.

In the Paris of Autumn 1949, there were two gods for intelligent young French and expatriates alike: Stalin and Sade. Stalin was then at the very peak of his popularity, and the French Communist Party, more than any other European Communist Party, assiduously followed the Stalinist line and utterly subjugated itself before Stalin's caprices and murderous manias (the French Party's leader, Jacques Duclos, once stated in a speech that he would be more than happy to castrate himself in public if 'The Boss' asked him to). In those postwar years, the French Communist Party almost seized power on several occasions, and Stalin already had a plan formulated to decimate the reactionary French bourgeoisie and send them in cattle-trucks to Magadan. Every young person's room in Paris had a poster of Stalin's glowering face on its wall, and, after a few months in the heated political atmosphere of Paris, Pot was no exception. However, it was to be his second influence, the Marquis de Sade, which would determine the future course of Pot's life and his vision for Cambodia. Like all young aristocrats with his French-influenced cultural upbringing, Pot had already read the poetry of Rimbaud and Baudelaire while still in Cambodia, and in Paris he now seized on the writings of Georges Bataille and Antonin Artaud (who had died in the year before his arrival in Paris). He soon began to talk to the other young Cambodians in Paris – most of whom he would later slaughter – of the compulsion for human life to revolve around the creation of an ecstatic Solar Anus, and the need to institute radical transformations in the matter of the human anatomy. But it was with the incendiary writings of the Marquis de Sade (who had died, locked-up in the Charenton asylum, in 1814) that Pot found his authentic source of inspiration, in the vision of a national state perpetually set into revolutionary turmoil by ever-escalating sexual deviance, but ruled with authoritarian power over life and death by one man. He told friends: 'What Sade attempted and was imprisoned as a madman for, I will put into practice.'

Along with absorbing these revolutionary ideas, Pot was also valuably spending his scholarship on a regime of carousing, whoring and drinking. From his bare room at 33 rue Letellier in the 15th arrondisement of the city, he would go out to the legendary 'bal musette', the Java dance-hall in the adjoining rue du Commerce, which, on frenetic weekend nights, was always full of vivacious young shopgirls who would be more than willing to offer their lubricated anuses for penetration in exchange for the price of several drinks. Pot often stopped off en route to the Java to chat amiably with the patrons of a tiny cafe at the corner of the rue Letellier and the rue du Commerce, the 'Rendez-vous des Amis', which the Vichard family (who, like most Parisian cafe owners, were from the Auvergne region of south-central France) ran from the mid-1940s until the early 2000s. Fifty years on, they remembered that the handsome and ever-smiling Pot always asked for a large glass of the expensive Dartigalongue armagnac, and they would often gently tease him about his reputation for buggering the neighbourhood girls. Since they were unable to pronounce Pot's given name, 'Saloth Sar', they simply called him 'Paul' (after his original religious calling), and, with the Auvergnat slang term for the anus being 'le pot', they naturally soon began to call him 'Paul Pot', which the friendly young Cambodian soon adopted and slightly adapted as his 'revolutionary' alias. ('Pot' also has the secondary connotation of 'pote', or 'pal' in English, and thus suited Pot's perpetually-beaming demeanour.) But the Java dance-hall was not the only destination of Pot's regular nocturnal sorties: he would often go to a cafe in the rue Gît-le-Coeur (a cafe so small and insignificant that it lacked even a name, although its position was significant, being situated only two doors along from the hotel which would serve as the Parisian centre of operations for the American writers William Burroughs and Brion Gysin, a decade later). At that cafe, a group of ten or twelve young Cambodian expatriates would huddle around a table and conduct political meetings, fulminating against the then-current usage of bacteriological warfare by the US army against Korean civilians in the ongoing Korean War, and vowing to one another that, on their return to their homeland, they would institute a Stalin-style dictatorship that would consign the French and Americans to history and get the Cambodian people finally on the road to revolutionary liberation, whether they liked it or not. Pot soon became the leader of this revolutionary cell which was always at pains not to attract the attention of the brutal French security police, who had been trained by the Nazi SS during the wartime German occupation of the city, and liked nothing better than to truncheon the heads of unruly young people with yellow or brown faces into a toothless, brain-damaged pulp of spurting blood, whether they were in Paris on official scholarships or not.

In the autumn of 1952, Pot's lucrative scholarship finally came to an end. The French government had expected him during his stay to gain expertise in radio technology which would have assisted the colonial French in their desire to dominate the Cambodian people more thoroughly through an efficient media system, but Pot had never attended a single lecture on the subject. And though he had learned fluent French and selectively absorbed aspects of French culture during his stay in Paris, that engagement with work such as Sade's would prove to be at the origins of his carnage-centred revolutionary regime when he seized power in Cambodia over twenty years later. Pot left France with increased hatred for the country's colonial stupidity and incompetence, and his only regret on boarding his ship to return to Cambodia in December 1952 (having outstayed his visa in order to conduct a final three-month-long non-stop session of sexual indulgence and revolutionary incitation) was that of leaving behind his Parisian life of all-out debauchery and revolutionary plotting, together with the regime of readily-available anal sex and succulent, skilled fellatio which the teenage girls of the 15th arrondisement had readily provided for their 'exotic' visitor. But above all, Pot's years in Paris had given him the unshakeable will for annihilation.

On the very same day that Pot's ship from France finally reached the port of Kompong Som in western Cambodia and he stepped out onto his homeland again, on 5 March 1953, Stalin succumbed to his fatal exertions in his villa in Kuntsevo. Now that the last of his idols was dead, Pot was aware that he could no longer hide in revolutionary rhetoric and provocation, and needed to start planning for the actual take-over of Cambodia. The French colonial power was now departing, but their stooge Norodom Sihanouk now ruled with the help of French 'advisors' and a brutal security police apparatus which enforced censorship and ensured that the Cambodian people remained cowed. Sihanouk was often distracted by the overpowering need for extended luxury shopping-trips to the USA and Europe (during which he repeatedly demonstrated his ability to spend the entire yearly domestic national income of Cambodia in the space of several hours), and his rule was erratic; he often switched allegiance at random between the USA (which, from the early 1960s, saw Cambodia as a valuable pawn in its growing conflict with neighbouring Vietnam) and Communist China, which used its patronage of Cambodia as a way of taunting its great rival, the Soviet Union. Faced with the danger of beginning his revolutionary mission in Phnom Penh under the eyes of Sihanouk's police, Pot decided to lay low. He took a job as a school-teacher, enabling him to recruit sixteen-year-old fighters for his revolutionary movement, which he named the 'Khmer Rouge' (evoking both the ancient Angkor Empire of Jayavarman VII and his hero, the 'red' tyrant, Stalin). Pot knew that only the very young had the will and the lack of compromise necessary to construct the Cambodia that he envisaged. Although Pot made several visits to the Communist party headquarters in Vietnam, he remained unwilling to ally his Khmer Rouge movement to other revolutionary groupings such as the Vietnamese Communist Party, which often limited themselves to what Pot viewed as mundane and futile aims of instituting equitable, peaceful societies – Pot's Cambodia was to be a far more ambitious concoction of carnage, sexual overkill and totalitarian power.

Pot spent his years at the Chamraon Vichea school in Phnom Penh reading Rimbaud to his entranced students, and covertly indoctrinating them into his vision for Cambodia; all of his students who managed to survive his years in power would remember the suave, handsome teacher, always dressed in a black short-sleeved shirt, reading in a hypnotic murmur, maintaining his perpetual smile and affable manner even when he introduced the subject of the necessity of exterminating a large part of the Cambodian people if they were to prove unresponsive to his project for the country. Soon, Pot had a large group of young followers, supplemented by a number of his fellow expatriates when they too returned from their stays in France (the French government abruptly discontinued its scholarships when it decided to abandon its colonial designs on Cambodia). To further the illusion that he was now a valuable and educated member of Cambodian society, Pot married a woman named Khieu Ponnary who was also engaged with the idea of a Cambodian revolution, but the extremity of Pot's vision (which he always liked to speak about at interminable length without interruption, as his supporters would discover to their cost after he seized power) soon proved mentally corrosive for her, driving her mad and white-haired overnight, and she was to spend the entirety of Pot's regime locked-away from public view, ranting that her husband was going to exterminate the whole world if he could.

In November 1963, Sihanouk took time away from his sophisticated shopping duties to order his police to orchestrate a mass crack-down on all dissident groups in Phnom Penh; this move led to the summary execution of a number of troublesome left-wing figures and also threatened to uncover Pot's group of covert revolutionaries. Pot told his followers that 'Sihanouk is more than 90 per cent paranoid due to all sorts of hedonism, corruption and debauchery'. The police closed further in on Pot, and finally he decided to flee the capital in order to pursue a strategy of guerrilla warfare, operating hit-and-run sabotage missions from the isolated jungles in the north-eastern periphery of the country, in the triangle of mountainous terrain close to Cambodia's borders with Vietnam and Laos. At first, Pot had only twelve followers, and the small band of revolutionaries were perpetually hunted and often surrounded by Sihanouk's army, escaping only with the help of local tribespeople – the Tapuon, Brao and Jarai tribes – who referred to Sihanouk as 'the Bloated Moron' and believed that any alternative was preferable to his corrupt regime. Sihanouk had now firmly allied himself with the USA, which was going all-out to decimate the North Vietnamese Communists, spraying them with napalm and committing repeated atrocities, massacres and sexual violations on Vietnamese civilians. Sihanouk had appointed a pro-US military general, Lon Nol, as the head of his government (over the coming years, Sihanouk and Lon Nol would sometimes shrewdly give the impression that they were opposed to one another or even adversaries, as a strategy to confuse the Cambodian dissident groups). Together, they authorized the infamous plan of the US President Richard Nixon and his Secretary of State, Henry Kissinger, to secretly bomb massive areas of the north-eastern regions of Cambodia, where a part of the North Vietnamese Army was hiding. In the resulting hell-fire of incineration bombs, Unit 731-derived bacteriological agents and napalm, which began in March 1969 and continued for an entire year, Pot and his followers had to be on the move constantly in order to avoid being carbonized. Hundreds of thousands of Cambodian tribespeople were killed by the US bombing, while the Vietnamese troops who were the ostensible target of the attacks largely survived by adroitly crossing back into Vietnam.

By the end of 1970, Pot had established a vast compound in the dense jungle alongside the border with Laos, where his own followers were in turn supported by the Tapuon, Brao and Jarai tribespeople. Two of the three tribes, the Brao and Jarai, were cannibals, and anyone who came near Pot's camp found themselves eviscerated and then eaten while still alive; thousands of severed heads were placed on poles to mark the boundaries of the compound. A trickle of deserters from the US Army attempted to ally themselves with Pot's Khmer Rouge forces, but Pot ordered them to undertake sabotage missions with the Tapuon tribesmen, who were both cannibals and necrophiles, and delighted in sodomizing the corpses of the renegade Americans before feasting on them. The primitive tribespeople pledged undying loyalty to Pot, and many of them would go on to serve as his bodyguards and trusted associates to the very end of his years in power. Pot was impressed that the tribespeople existed without using money, operated as incestuous free-sex collectives, hated going near cities (which they perceived as devilish) and had only hazy conceptions of time and space; he decided to incorporate elements of their lifestyle into his own vision for Cambodia. Each evening, Pot would broadcast a three-hour-long radio transmission to the Khmer Rouge units that were operating away from his main compound; many of his pronouncements, intercepted and transcribed into English by anonymous US Army radio engineers, possess a harsh poetry of breathless horror that prefigures Marlon Brando's improvisations in Francis Ford Coppola's film *Apocalypse Now!*. Pot declares that: 'We are poised on the blade of the knife: utter failure on one side, the glorious unknown on the other. If we fail, we deserve to be slaughtered like pigs, but if we win, we will be doing the slaughtering, and none of our enemies will escape with their throats intact.' At the end of the transmissions, he insistently incites his followers to 'Kill them! Every last one! Kill them all!'. Pot's nightly rambling pep-talks to the Khmer Rouge reconnaissance units carry the authentic voice of atrocity.

Over the early 1970s, Pot's revolutionary army gathered in strength and began to recruit intellectuals from the Cambodian cities who had heard about Pot's 'pure revolution of fire and slaughtered meat'; more and more Khmer Rouge compounds sprang up throughout eastern Cambodia, and Pot spent his time travelling between them, preparing his forces for the eventual assault on Phnom Penh and his seizure of power. Perversely, the factor which finally enabled Pot for the first time to confront Sihanouk and Lon Nol's forces head-on was the US's botched attempt to decimate the Khmer Rouge by bombing their compounds – by this point, the US forces had become so enraged at their evident humiliation and incipient defeat by the Vietnamese that they now turned in desperation to the Khmer Rouge as a substitute target. Pot's army had become, as US army chiefs put it, 'the only game in town'. In the five months from March 1973, the US Air Force dropped a quarter of a million tons of incendiary bombs on Cambodia with wild inaccuracy; very few of the Khmer Rouge were killed, but over three hundred thousand civilians were carbonized or blown to fragments by the American weaponry. The US's plan to decimate the Khmer Rouge backfired spectacularly. Exasperated with Sihanouk's corruption and his alliance with the US forces, many thousands of young Cambodians now rushed to join Pot's forces, as utterly committed recruits to his radical vision for their country. Sihanouk panicked and began to switch alliances so rapidly and erratically between his US and Chinese patrons that eventually he was deserted by both of them. Pot could now begin to instigate the Cambodian Year Zero.

Pot massed his forces in eastern Cambodia and then ordered them to rampage towards Phnom Penh in June 1973, terrifying the peasant population as the ferocious young male and female fighters (with an average age of sixteen) charged through the rural landscape of rice paddies. But the US saturation bombing of the country was still going on at that time, and many of Pot's units were hit and destroyed by airfire as they approached the capital. On the ground, Lon Nol's US-trained army succeeded in beating back the offensive. In July, with monsoon storms raging around the bloody battles, Pot (who always stayed at a safe distance from the fighting) instructed his troops to stage a temporary retreat. In March 1974, after the US bombing campaign had ended, he ordered a second onslaught, but still Lon Nol's army (whose soldiers knew what was coming if they lost) managed to hold the Khmer Rouge back, with hand-to-hand machete fighting and horrendous casualties on either side. During the final months of 1974, the Khmer Rouge finally succeeded in encircling the capital and cut all of its communications to the outside world. Then, on 1 January 1975, Pot's Khmer Rouge began their offensive for total power for the third time.

THE KHMER ROUGE TAKE-OVER

The battle for Phnom Penh went on for over three months. During that same period, all of the other major cities of Cambodia also came under assault by the secondary units of Pot's forces. Throughout that time, Pot himself stayed safely hidden in the forests of the eastern region of Mondulkiri, surrounded by four thousand of his cannibalistic tribesmen bodyguards, who were ready to protect him to the death if the assault went badly and Lon Nol's forces staged a counter-attack. But Lon Nol, as an authentically incompetent stooge of the USA, could see the situation was going rapidly downhill for his young army, and was already arranging his helicopter airlift out of Phnom Penh and planning the details of his luxurious retirement in Florida. As a result, the two armies of desperate sixteen-year-old fighters faced one another on the dusty plains and swamplands surrounding the city without commanders or orders (except for Pot's injunction to 'exterminate every last one of them!', which he repeated each night in ranting

Cambodian soldier maimed by the Khmer Rouge

radio broadcasts to his troops) and the battle turned into a merciless bloodbath, with huge casualties inflicted on either side. For the first two months, the groups of young fighters tore into one another relentlessly, and the ground around the city became saturated with the decomposing bodies – riddled with high-calibre machine-gun fire or sliced apart with machete blows – of both sides' fighters.

At least a third of Pot's forces comprised sixteen-year-old rebel girls, who rode around the combat zone at speed on motorcycles, machine-guns and machetes strapped to their backs, picking off Lon Nol's dazed troops and decapitating

them where they stood before wildly roaring off towards their next target. All of them were ready to sacrifice their lives for Pot's great vision of Cambodia's future. Pot had instilled in them the crucial element of sexual seduction in guerrilla warfare, and one of their favourite strategies was to disguise themselves as peasant girls and place an explosive charge deep in their anuses. Then, when Lon Nol's moronic boy-soldiers – desperate for the consolations of arbitrary and violent pillage in the lulls between the fighting – attempted to anally rape or fistfuck the guerrilla fighters in peasant disguise, they would find themselves suddenly minus their sexual organs or forearms. (The girls usually survived the bloody detonation of their anuses, and went on to display their lacerations as a courageous badge of honour and a tribute to Pot's genius.) A number of reckless journalists and photographers attempted to capture the ferocity of the battle for Phnom Penh, and a few rare photographs survived of the results of such strategies. However, Pot fiercely despised journalists and all media in general, and ordered that the battlefields should be 'cleansed of those poisonous mosquitoes' – the journalists soon found themselves the massacred target of the Khmer Rouge's crazed machete charges, and the assault on Phnom Penh resulted in one of the highest death tolls inflicted on journalists in the history of twentieth-century conflict.

By the middle of April 1975, Lon Nol's remaining troops were exhausted – many of them had lost one or more limbs, and the first pummelling storms of the rainy season had reduced their US-sponsored uniforms to rags. They had been pushed back to the very edges of Phnom Penh itself. Pot ordered a terminal slaughter for 17 April, and the massed Khmer Rouge fighters, aided by Pot's salivating tribesmen, tore through the scattered bands of dispirited fighters around the peripheries of the city, slaughtering them to the last boy and girl in the middle of a hot dawn rainstorm. When the Khmer Rouge had avalanched their way through Lon Nol's army, all that was left were hundreds of steaming carcasses without heads, most of them reduced to butchered fragments of flesh. Lon Nol now decided that it was time to flee and ordered his helicopter to prepare for take-off, although Sihanouk, paralysed with terror, refused to move

Opposite: Teenage rebel girls of the Khmer Rouge

and remained in his palace, surrounded by his courtesans and servants. Lon Nol's helicopter took off from the roof of his headquarters as the first Khmer Rouge troops entered the city. By the next day, he was in exile in Miami, sunning himself by his swimming-pool at the salubrious villa provided for him by the USA. Meanwhile, the sixteen-year-old Khmer Rouge fighters entered Phnom Penh in absolute silence. At first, the inhabitants of the city crowded round them in celebration, thanking them for ending the corrupt regime of Sihanouk and Lon Nol. But the gun-toting and grim-faced Khmer Rouge fighters pushed them aside in contempt, and the five hundred thousand inhabitants of Phnom Penh began to realise that this was not an innocuous coup which would leave their lives essentially unchanged. Something very strange was unfolding. Already, Pot's young revolutionaries were starting to shoot people at random, to close down shops and to burn money. For Pot, all of the urban inhabitants of Phnom Penh were 'enemies' who had refused to ally themselves with him in his great vision for Cambodia. And as 'enemies', they had to be obliterated.

With Phnom Penh firmly in his grip, Pot now revealed the first part of his great vision for Cambodia. All of the other Cambodian cities had fallen to his forces in the preceding days. For the time being, he remained hidden in the jungles of Mondulkiri (fearing, above all, that he might be assassinated before he could put his grand project fully into operation), and relayed his orders by radio to his commanders in the cities. Influenced by the hatred of cities of his loyal tribespeople, he had decided that all of the cities of Cambodia were to be partly destroyed and emptied of their populations. Although his ideal plan would have been to destroy every city down to its very ashes, he knew that this would consume too much time and detract from the other elements of his great plan, and so he contented himself with ordering the destruction of only parts of each city. In Phnom Penh, all shops, stalls, markets and banks were set alight to erase all traces of consumerism. Every school, college and library was burned down to expunge all evidence of writing and all vestiges of pre-existent knowledge. By the afternoon of 17 March, the sky above Phnom Penh was streaked with towering flames and columns of black smoke, and the terrified population were cowering in abject fear in their houses and shacks.

The entire population of Phnom Penh was to be expelled from the city. The first part of Pot's great plan was that these urban 'enemies' would eventually be brutally massacred by overwork, beatings and starvation in the rice-fields of the country; this would have the added bonus, at least initially, of generating extra food supplies for the Khmer Rouge. Pot ordered that these despised city-dwellers should be sent on forced death-marches into the countryside; anyone who resisted or lagged behind would be slaughtered. They would have only the minutest possibility of survival by becoming super-quota workers. The authentic peasants of Cambodia, on the other hand, met with Pot's approval, since they had genuinely loathed the sophisticated fop Sihanouk's squandering of the country's wealth, and had often helped out the Khmer Rouge revolutionaries with gifts of food or shelter during their long years on the run from Sihanouk's forces. On the evening of 17 April, the entire population of Phnom Penh was ordered out of their houses and shacks; those who tried to remain hidden or declined to join in with the revolutionary upheaval of Cambodia were gunned down on the spot by Pot's sullen sixteen-year-old cadres. All possessions had to be abandoned. The first death marches began immediately, with one hundred thousand shop-keepers and service-industry workers dispatched on foot towards the far north and east of the country. By the time the bedraggled columns finally reached their destinations, hallucinating with starvation and exhaustion, only thirty thousand remained alive. (Among the victims who dropped dead en route was Pot's once-beautiful courtesan sister, Saroeun, then in her mid-fifties, who had been working as a royal procuress until the arrival of her brother's revolutionary army.) The remainder of the city's population had to camp out in the plains surrounding Phnom Penh, often among the fast-putrefying carcasses of Lon Nol's decimated army, in order to await Pot's further orders.

Six days later, on 23 April 1975, Pot decided that it was now safe for him to enter the capital himself and to view the initial results of his revolution. His bodyguards drove him in an armoured jeep into the city past the swathes of massacred soldiers and the hundreds of thousands of city-dwellers whose fate hung on his caprice. Pot had decided to remain anonymous for the time being – the future of his regime would vitally depend on its aura of mystery and impenetrability. Surrounded by his bodyguards, Pot surveyed his revolutionary city as they drove at night through the deserted boulevards of Phnom Penh with its vast, luxurious villas built by the French colonials at the turn of the century. They roared by the royal palace, where Sihanouk (who knew of Pot only vaguely, as one of the myriad of subversives he had ordered executed or hunted down in 1963), almost comatose with sheer terror, awaited his fate under the new regime that had usurped his power. Pot had been absent from Phnom Penh for twelve years, and was now fifty years old; his years on the run, lurking in disease-ridden jungles and dodging US napalm conflagrations, eating a diet of large, indigestible insects and sleeping no more than an hour a night in order always to be ready to move on to the next hide-out, had deeply marked him. He was no longer the suave and handsome revolutionary who had returned from Paris in 1953; he now embodied more than ever his great plan for Cambodia, and was determined to carry it through immediately. Pot was now a walking force of stark death who lived and breathed genocide.

Despite the hardships of the previous decade, Pot still presented an affable demeanour to those around him, and was never seen without his beaming smile. He was now permanently wracked with chronic intestinal pain from his jungle diet of non-nutritious insect carapaces, but even when Pot was doubled-over with intestinal agony and barking out deafening blasts of flatulence, those who observed him in his first days of revolutionary glory never saw the smile leave his face. The loneliness of power afflicted him, and Pot momentarily considered handing over his authority to someone younger and with less addled internal organs, but decided that he would have to wield absolute power himself. During the first years of his regime, he would often remain hidden in the background, taking and then immediately resigning official posts in the Khmer Rouge organization, in order to screen the level of ultimate power he held. And, despite his physical frailty, Pot remained compelled to execute his vision for Cambodia and make it a reality. Although he had now thoroughly subjugated the country to his will, there remained an even vaster project still to undertake: the unbreakable alliance of murderous dictatorial power with the total dissolution of family structures and the institution of a national state based entirely on relentless sexual obliteration.

Pot took the first steps towards distancing his new country from the corruption of the rest of the world by instituting a new time. Time itself had stopped dead at the moment when Pot's forces had occupied and annulled the Cambodian cities. Like the Roman Emperor Commodus, who decreed that all time existed only through his own divine authority, and had to be known by his citizens as 'The Time of Commodus', Pot ordered that 17 April 1975, the day on which the initial stage of his revolution had succeeded, would be Day Zero of Year Zero. All of the territories around Cambodia were erased from maps of the country, so that it appeared to be floating free within an immense black void. Pot also formally ordered the end of money in Cambodia: all banknotes and coins were to be destroyed, together with all of the possessions which the citizens of Phnom Penh had been ordered to leave behind when they were expelled from the city. All knowledge prior to the accession to power of Pot was similarly negated and utterly wiped away, together with all books and media. The first piece of knowledge, the first sensory input and the first sexual impulse to be experienced by the new inhabitants of Cambodia would all be magnanimously gifted to them from the glorious world of Pot.

Among all of the instituted negation of his first revolutionary edicts, Pot aberrantly slipped in one capricious promise which indicated the degree to which his noxious insect diet of the previous decade had afflicted him. He vowed to the revolutionary inhabitants of Cambodia that there would be a significant increase in the amount of pudding that was to be their right: 'In Year Two [1977], there will be two desserts per week. In Year Three [1978], there will be one dessert every two days. Then, in Year Four [1979], every true revolutionary will receive one dessert per day.' For the wild and ravenous sixteen-year-old cadres of the Khmer Rouge, the announcement of the vast augmentation of desserts (which never actually materialized) was a major cause for celebration. However, the news presented only limited interest for the hundreds of thousands of former city-dwellers who had been camped outside the capital for the past week, and were now being corralled into collective work units and allocated hard-labour duties in the areas surrounding Phnom Penh, under the harsh supervision of the authentic peasants. Those ex-metropolitan inhabitants, now stigmatized and collectively renamed '17 April People' to indicate their criminal allegiance to the pre-revolutionary form of Cambodia, would not be receiving even the promise of future desserts – they were subsisting on prairie grass and on a minuscule quantity of stale millet and polluted water each day.

Pot himself had taken up residence in the deserted city, recreating the form of his jungle compound by fencing off five of the outbuildings of the royal palace, and giving instructions to his bodyguards to shoot on sight anyone who came near. Pot was accompanied by the gang of henchmen – principally, Ta Mok, Son Sen, Ieng Sary and Nuon Chea – who comprised his subordinates in the Khmer Rouge leadership and to whom he could delegate revolutionary tasks: all of them subjugated themselves utterly before Pot's authority. Several of Pot's henchmen, such as Ieng Sary, had been his covert companions in Paris, in the cafe in the rue Gît-le-Coeur, twenty-five years earlier, and had spent the intervening decades laying low and idly 'waiting for the revolution to reach fruition' (without the determination of Pot, they would have lived out their entire lives in provincial backwaters, hiding from Sihanouk's police). Other henchmen, such as Ta Mok, were brutal thugs from the Cambodian criminal underworld who had seen the rise of the Khmer Rouge as a valuable opportunity to participate in the mass pursuit of acts of gratuitous carnage and terror. Pot settled into a luxurious pavilion in the centre of his compound, where he would receive the nightly visits of his adept sixteen-year-old revolutionary cadres of both sexes; after twelve sex-deprived years in the jungle, where the removal of any clothes invited lethal bites from brain-rotting parasites, Pot needed both to make up for lost time, and also to intensively pursue his experimentation into the extreme neural and sensory dimensions of the sexual act, solely for the future benefit of his people. Pot's private chefs provided him with three desserts each day, but otherwise he lived with great frugality.

Once the situation had stabilized in Cambodia and the inhabitants of the newly-instituted hard-labour collectives were busily working themselves to death, Pot decided to tour the country to check that everything was in revolutionary order. He travelled by train on the one railway line that had survived the US bombing of the country, along with his deputy, Nuon Chea, who undertook many of the practical arrangements for Pot's genocide (Nuon Chea always had to sit in the train seat behind Pot to demonstrate his subordinate status). Pot was able to travel in secret, since he had still not revealed his identity to the Cambodian people – all they knew was that the country was now ruled by the 'Great Apparatus', and even when he finally announced in October 1977 that he, Pot, was the Heart of the Revolution, it left everyone baffled and very few people connected Pol Pot with the minor aristocrat Saloth Sar who had abruptly disappeared in the early 1960s. In the first years of his regime, only the Khmer Rouge veterans could identify Pot by sight. Pot visited the many labour camps dotted around Phnom Penh to watch the backbreaking manual work being undertaken by the starving former-inhabitants of the capital, who were regularly castigated and beaten with clubs by their peasant supervisors. He incited his devoted revolutionary cadres to construct more and more of what he called 'annihilation zones'. Throughout all of his excursions around central Cambodia during his first year in power, Pot maintained his ever-smiling demeanour. Even when he ordered summary executions of slacking workers, or addressed bitter admonitions to the now-exhausted ex-cosmopolitans, as they dug three-metre-deep trenches in liquid mud and carried huge blocks of concrete from place to place, Pot kept smiling among the horror.

The expelled inhabitants of the cities now slept packed-together in vast plywood dormitories which they had to build themselves from scratch, alongside the fields where they worked; the one meal they received a day, consisting of a spoonful of watery millet-porridge mixed with grass and weeds, was eaten communally. All families had been arbitrarily broken up, with their members sent to different zones of the country, and all of their property had been confiscated and destroyed. This forcible collectivization of Cambodia also extended to those inhabitants of the country whom Pot was not intending to massacre (or, at least, not for the time being). Pot had decreed that the entire population of Cambodia (including himself) would wear a stylish suit of black pyjamas which he designed himself, in a hardwearing mixture of cotton and jute-cloth. All other clothes were burned. Apart from the reprehensible '17 April' ex-urban people who, with few exceptions, were destined for death by work-related exhaustion or brutal beatings, Pot intended that all of the new inhabitants of Cambodia would form one great collective, united in their revolutionary ambitions. He decided to rename the country 'Democratic Kampuchea' (the name 'Kampuchea', like that of the Khmer Rouge, resonates with the great twelfth-century Angkor Empire of Jayavarman VII) as a sign of those egalitarian desires. Kampuchea would be democratic in the sense that Pot would regularly allow full and fair democratic elections, as long as he (in his guise as the 'Great Apparatus') was the only candidate and no-one even considered voting for anybody else, on pain of immediate death by torture.

No resistance whatsoever emerged to Pot's great project within the country itself. The only element of the population that had ever demonstrated any resistance in recent years had been the peasants, and since Pot accorded them a high degree of 'authenticity' and allowed them the brutal pleasures of capricious power in their supervision of the contemptible ex-urban people, they were now fully contented. The only potential problem would arise when the expansion of their crop-yield, for which they now possessed a vast slave-labour force, began to diminish again as the '17 April' people slowly worked themselves into oblivion. Outside Cambodia, resistance was also negligible. Three weeks after Pot had seized power in Phnom Penh (causing the US Embassy staff to follow Lon Nol in a final helicopter evacuation), the US-controlled South Vietnamese capital of Saigon had finally fallen to the rampaging North Vietnamese Communist forces, resulting in the US's ultimate humiliation of the 1970s. As a result, the American government now had little enthusiasm for further interference in South-East Asia. Cambodia's former colonial 'protectors', the French, had finally learned their lesson after their own abject colonial defeats in South-East Asia and in North Africa, and now preferred to perceive South-East Asia as the innocuous setting for 'exotic' soft-core film pornography such as *Emmanuelle* rather than as the venue for genocidal massacres and haywire atrocities. The only possible threat remaining to Pot's edenic regime was that from the adjoining country of Vietnam, which had a centuries-long history of invading Cambodia: now that it had successfully repelled and belittled the mighty USA, it had started to eye the gem-rich territory of Cambodia and the unexploited oil resources off its western seacoast. But, for the moment, Pot's sole remaining dilemma lay in deciding whether or not he should execute the regal fop Sihanouk, who was under house arrest in his palace, still awaiting his fate. Finally, Pot decided that he should keep the terrified Sihanouk alive, provisionally, in case he should come in useful in the future. Even so, Sihanouk was 'finished', as Pot told his henchmen. Like the inhabitants of Magadan, he could be killed at any time, but would never know exactly when.

Although his revolution was developing smoothly, Pot began to have misgivings and new preoccupations at the end of his first year in power. He would soon have to begin the detailed planning for the second phase of his great project – the alliance of sexual and dictatorial revolutions – and believed that in order for it to be executed with the necessary purity and lack of compromise, he would need to root out all those who were not thoroughly committed to his plan: these were 'traitors' and 'enemies', within the Khmer Rouge itself, who deserved a far more terrible death than the '17 April' people. He would also need to eliminate a number of the Khmer Rouge veterans who might compromise the dense secrecy through which his regime operated, thereby making his own position of supreme power vulnerable to being usurped. Pot was also increasingly preoccupied with a group of fifteen thousand of the ex-urban people whom he had ordered to be set aside from the rest, since he had reserved a particular fate for them. These were the Cambodian intellectuals, whom Pot viewed as the servile receptacles of European cultural influence. For the special attention which he needed to devote to these 'problem' groups, Pot began to contemplate the construction of a suitable facility where they could all be 'sent to study' before being 'smashed'.

THE NECESSARY EXTERMINATION OF ALL INTELLECTUALS

Pol Pot's philosophy – from the first to last moments of his regime of carnage – was the philosophy of death. Although his regime was sometimes superficially dubbed a 'Communist' one by the outside world (this was one of the reasons why the USA had attempted to saturation-bomb the Khmer Rouge into oblivion in 1973), Pot's knowledge of Communist doctrine was peripheral at best. He often referred vaguely in his speeches to an important figure named 'Max Lenin', but any of his associates who tried delicately to suggest to Pot that he had scrambled together Karl Marx and Vladimir Lenin would usually find a searing blowtorch had dissolved their facial features by the end of the day. However, from the time of his arrival in Paris in 1949, Pot had always been attracted by the acts of Stalin, in particular his determination, on the most gratuitous of whims, to send fourteen million blameless people to their icy and brutal deaths in the extermination zone of Magadan; he was also captivated by Stalin's ability to order (on the most aberrant of caprices) entire populations to be moved from one end of the Soviet Union to the other, with the resulting death-marches and agonizing cattle-truck journeys also resulting in millions of fatalities. Pot also admired Stalin's capacity to blithely send even his closest associates off to the depths of the Lubyanka torture chambers whenever he was struck by the slightest suspicion that they might (at some point in the future) become traitors or 'wreckers'. In the Soviet Union, in the years following Stalin's death, his reputation suffered because his great obsession with wanton mass carnage had gone out of fashion; but for Pot, now in his own position of supreme power, Stalin appeared more than ever to be his authentic guiding light. Like Stalin, he had even managed to drive his own wife into a state of raving insanity (although Pot's mad wife Khieu Ponnary never actually committed suicide, as Stalin's did, and even outlived her husband, still ranting about Pot's tyranny to the end). Along with the twelfth-century Angkor Emperors whose ambitious experiments in divine sexual cruelty he prized highly, Pot also looked back – in formulating his philosophy of death – to the seminal Emperors of Imperial Rome, most especially Caligula, who ordered all of the great philosophers of his time to appear before him and then had burning pokers rammed into their anuses, and on hearing their tortured screams, commented: 'Now that is true philosophy'.

The particular focus of Pot's wrath was directed towards Cambodia's intellectuals, writers and journalists, who had slavishly supported the corruption of Sihanouk and his predecessors, and – for most of the twentieth century – had also attempted to convince the population of Cambodia that they should subjugate themselves utterly to the colonial and cultural power of France. Before the arrival of Pot's regime, the pretentious proponents of this colonial envy had dreamed above all of leaving the dusty Cambodian capital behind and making trips to Paris, the 'City of Light', and even of living there (although the few intellectuals who actually made the journey usually discovered that they were habitually treated with racial contempt by the French population and often found themselves being clubbed into Parisian gutters by its fascist-trained police). Pot valued only those French writers who had turned in incandescent fury and denunciation against their own country, such as Sade; he viewed the Cambodian intellectuals' idolization of France as incontrovertible evidence of their criminal treachery, which could only be fairly punished by the unmitigated mass-torture and wholesale extermination of all of its perpetrators. A further crime of the Cambodian intelligentsia was its reluctance to support the Khmer Rouge during their long years of harassed exile in the Cambodian jungles; while Pot had been rationing himself to two dung-beetles a days in the monsoon-sodden jungle in the early 1970s, the Cambodian intellectuals had been busily cramming *foie gras* and oysters into their salivating mouths on the veranda of Phnom Penh's 'Le Royal' hotel while reading turgid novels by Alain Robbe-Grillet. Now, they would have to pay in full for those crimes against his revolution, and Pot was devising a special punishment to fit the gravity of their misdeeds.

In order to expand the scope of his regime of terror and annihilation, Pot depended absolutely on his army of ferocious sixteen-year-old fighters, who – at the moment of Pot's seizure of power in Phnom Penh – had become its official police force, charged with dispatching the city's hapless population on their death marches and with guarding the Cambodian ex-intelligentsia until Pot had finalized the suitable medium of their demise. Only the young had the iron resolve and the lack of compromise necessary to undertake the foundation of Pot's revolutionary state; they also possessed the will, stamina and imagination to carry forward the radical sexual experimentation which the 'Great Apparatus', Pot, would soon demand of them. Pot's young Khmer Rouge fighters were ready to die to safeguard the revolution and its instigator; most of them only rarely caught glimpses of the suave and black-clad Pot, during his rare public appearances, but those young revolutionaries who had mastered particularly adroit sexual skills could be summoned at any time of the night to Pot's palatial compound to provide demonstrations of their sensorial aptitudes. The only potential problem for Pot in maintaining the pure ferocity of his cadres was that, once Year Zero had moved on to Year One, those fighters would no longer have the sheer cruelty of youth and might begin to compromise the revolution; at that moment, they themselves would necessarily have to be mercilessly culled by a new generation of sixteen-year-old revolutionaries.

Pot's revolutionary vision for Cambodia demanded that all independent thought and action on the part of his population merited immediate death: only he, Pot, had the authority to devise and formulate methods of human destruction, to order the division of the country into forced-labour and murder zones, and to decide on the nature of time and space, and of sex and death. But although thought itself was viewed as a malevolent and counter-revolutionary act in Pot's Cambodia (thought might lead on to ideas, and then eventually to the development of another criminal band of intellectuals), his population possessed the absolute freedom to receive whatever sensory stimuli they might choose to, however aberrant, perverse and deviant those sensory strata might be. Unfortunately, apart from the Khmer Rouge cadres and the dull-witted peasants, very few of the population of Cambodia had the leisure time necessary to enjoy their new-found sensory liberation, since the primary experiences of the millions of fast-expiring '17 April' people were now those of abject starvation, of vicious beatings and violations from their peasant masters, and of gruelling servitude to the ultimate will of Pot. Even so, Pot's great philosophy of death allowed them the total freedom to experience whatever individual sensations they were able to, in the short intervals before their collective deaths. Pot's Sade-inspired revolution was to be corporeal and sensory, with the mental outlawed and simply wiped from the face of the earth.

All of Pot's associates (or 'brothers', as they called one another) in the Khmer Rouge leadership were required to display servile loyalty towards the 'Great Apparatus', Pot, although Pot himself continued to remain hidden for most of the time, through his desire to avoid assassination and to consolidate the dense aura of mystery through which his power operated. When it became evident that Pot was planning to gratuitously order the torture and execution of those of his co-leaders whom he might arbitrarily stigmatize as 'traitors', his associates' manifestations of servility intensified, mixed with fear, and the Khmer Rouge inner circle – Ta Mok, Son Sen, Khek Penn and Nuon Chea – jostled with one another in their efforts to formulate phrases that exalted Pot's great leadership: 'Brother Number One', 'The Magnificent Organ', and 'The Blinding Light of Revolutionary Illumination'. The Cambodian peasants, too, idolized Pot for overthrowing the pompous fop Sihanouk and for giving them such a vast work-force, which they could lethally overstretch and brutally abuse at will; but they, too, began to develop a dread of Pot's power when it dawned on them that, once all of the '17 April' people had been massacred, Pot's headlong desire to inflict annihilation might well turn towards them. Similarly, the young Khmer Rouge revolutionaries who had fought for Pot and captured Phnom Penh on his behalf were now starting to become uneasy, since it was palpably clear that their lives were infinitely expendable and replaceable. In the world of Pot, there was no escape. Servility itself was a crime of weakness punishable by death; and doubt or resistance were crimes of treachery equally punishable by death. Whichever way the population of Cambodia turned, they came up against the face of death. Pot himself let it be known in his radio broadcasts that his well-coiffured head now possessed many eyes, all powerfully trained on his people, with every eye ready to launch death upon them.

A crucial part of Pot's philosophy of death lay in its relentless indoctrination of previously innocuous elements of the population to take on the status of merciless killers, ready to inflict acts of terminal cruelty on ostensibly-blameless strangers. The Cambodian peasantry, although deeply surly and churlish, were not usually murderous by temperament, preferring to take out their engrained frustrations about their execrably low social status via an intensive regime of bestial sex with water-buffaloes and other amenable rural animals. One of the ways in which Pot accomplished the necessary training of the dull-witted peasantry in gratuitous carnage was to send large groups of the 'April 17' people to areas of the country – such as Kratie and Ratanakiri – that had been decimated in 1969 and 1973 by the US bombing, which the peasants' great enemy Sihanouk had reputedly sponsored; the former city-people were viewed by the peasants as primarily responsible, because of their support for the regal dandy Sihanouk, for the repeated napalming, vaporization and incineration of their families and neighbours by the US Air Force's saturation firestorms. As a result, when they had the ex-urbanites under their power, the peasantry were usually ready to work them to death at the optimum speed, to club into oblivion those recalcitrant former city-dwellers who baulked at working twenty-two-hour days in the muddy fields, and to perform the more capricious acts of atrocity which the Khmer Rouge cadres controlling their regions instructed the peasants to undertake. The Khmer Rouge themselves preferred simply to slaughter the exhausted and expended groups of 'April 17' people with blasts of gun-fire, and left the more frenetic bludgeoning and clubbing to the peasants.

The enmity of the peasants towards the former city-dwellers was exacerbated by the urbanites' sheer inability to work as hard as the peasants themselves. In their air-conditioned offices, banks and stores in the Cambodian cities, the 'April 17' people had been habituated to a far more leisurely rate of work, often with four-hour lunch-breaks. Thousands of them had functioned as royal bureaucrats, employed solely in dispatching Sihanouk's shopping orders to the couture houses of Paris and Milan; others, engaged in post-colonial business dealings with French gem-mining companies, had never even seen a peasant before Pot's revolution of 17 April 1975. Their new lives of permanent toil in the waterlogged fields – regularly covered in deluges of animal excrement as they shouldered the stubborn rice-ploughing water-buffaloes along, or futilely digging three-metre-deep trenches in liquid mud – proved too much of a humiliation for them, and they often pleaded with their peasant masters to kill them on the spot. The peasants also faced other pressures which led them to take out their frustrations on their new slaves. Even though he had provided his peasantry with a vast workforce, Pot had simultaneously exacted vast increases in the amount of rice and other crops which he expected the peasants to produce. According to Pot's first revolutionary Five-Year-Plan, the country's rice yields would need to double in each of the first three years, and then triple in the final two years. With the advent of collectivization, the peasants would no longer be able to keep a percentage of the crops for themselves (the Khmer Rouge cadres took away all of the crops immediately after the harvests), and they could no longer pursue their favourite occupations of hoarding and counting money, since all money had now been abolished. And, worst of all, the rice and millet harvests in Year Zero and Year One were the worst ever recorded, blighted by terrible insect-storms and monsoons. The peasants' new deity, Pot, began to take on the form of a malign god who had cursed their lives.

Many of the participants of the numerous death-marches ordered by Pot never reached their new peasant masters. Pot – taking his cue from his great idol, Stalin, who liked nothing better than to uproot vast populations from the hot semi-desert regions of the south-western Soviet Union and dispatch them to an icy nameless zone fifteen thousand miles away to the north-east – often capriciously changed his mind about the destinations of the death columns. Straggling lines of fifty thousand famished urbanites would walk from the outskirts of Phnom Penh to the mountainous Stung Treng region on the frontier with Laos, without food or water, only to be told by the Khmer Rouge cadres there that the 'Great Apparatus' had decreed that they had criminally gone in the wrong direction and had to set off immediately for the opposite periphery of the country, to Sisophon, near the malaria-infested border with Thailand. Many of the shattered '17 April' people would simply drop dead in desperation at the news. By the end of Pot's first year in power, over half a million former city-dwellers were still randomly crisscrossing the country, their columns going nowhere and gradually diminishing, as more and more of the participants expired from starvation and exhaustion. Few Khmer Rouge guards were needed to accompany the death columns. They knew that there was no escape from the grip of Pot, and they marched until they died.

Once the criminal '17 April' people had been thoroughly scythed into oblivion, Pot's Cambodian society was unrecognizably transformed from its position before his murderous seizure of power. Almost all of the levels of that previous society had been wiped away: the French-controlled bankers and financial officials, the addled aristocracy, the wealthy owners of monasteries with their lucrative networks of temples and their self-flagellating monks, the royal hangers-on and courtesans, the bureaucrats and the remaining die-hard colonials. Pot's philosophy of death required that a vast obliteration of excess elements needed to be mercilessly undertaken before he could even begin his true work. The only people to survive in the revolutionary eden that resulted from Pot's all-out strategy of social slaughter would be the active contributors to his great plan – the authentic peasants, the wild sixteen-year-old revolutionary cadres, and Pot himself: Democratic Kampuchea's 'Brother Number One' – all of them clad in black pyjamas and toting fully-loaded machine-guns in case of any treacherous counter-attack by the 'megacolonialist' hordes of the USA, Britain and France. With all of the tainted traces of money, time and knowledge destroyed, Pot could begin to envisage a far vaster project for Cambodia, welding together the sexual and totalitarian organs of his revolution into an aberrantly pulsing mutant body. After that, the final stage in his great philosophical vision for Cambodia was to be an all-consuming genocidal implosion that would suck in and decimate not only Cambodia, but the entire world: the terminal world revolution.

By the early summer of 1976, Pot's Cambodia was in utter turmoil. The mass-killings of '17 April' people, through overwork and peasant beatings, had now been substantially accomplished, with over two million fatalities. Hundreds of thousands of additional urbanites had been lethally driven into the ground by gruelling death-marches. Both the Cambodian peasants and the Khmer Rouge leadership were now more than ever fully-subjugated to the will of Pot, trapped into a spiral of ever-greater servitude and of raw terror at the near-certainty of their own imminent deaths. And Cambodia had succeeded in isolating itself entirely from the negated outside world, with the result that it had begun again from zero and now possessed its own unique dimensions of time and space. Finally, it had divested itself entirely of the twin malevolent presences that might have impeded the purity of Pot's revolution: knowledge and money. Now that his great project for Cambodia was fully underway, Pot could turn his attention to the moment he had been waiting for: the mandatory 'smashing' and extermination of the conceited intellectuals who had failed to support the establishment of his regime, together with all those among the Khmer Rouge revolutionaries who might at some point in the future potentially betray him and therefore needed to be excised now. It was time for them all to be 'sent to study' at Tuol Sleng.

TUOL SLENG: DEATH FACILITY S-21

Pot ordered that a large college building, on Tuol Sleng ('Poison Hill') in the empty capital's southern suburbs, be converted into a vast torture and extermination centre, comprising hundreds of cells and a series of heavily-barred rooms equipped with blowtorches, scalpels, electric prods and prongs, cages of starving rats, and a vast array of blunt instruments. The building was around ten miles from an expanse of abandoned fields, known as Choeung Ek, which had been assigned for the disposal of the finished products of Pot's atrocities. Tuol Sleng was to be the venue for Pot's great plan to provide 'special treatment' for the fifteen thousand intellectuals he had set aside from the city-people's death-marches, together with all of his 'enemies' and 'traitors' among the ranks of his Khmer Rouge followers. The facility was converted for use over the late summer of 1976 and was ready for operation in the autumn of that year. Tuol Sleng was an anonymous Bauhaus-style construction built from shoddy concrete-blocks and bricks, in the final years of French colonial power, already falling into dilapidation after its occupants had been expelled in the previous year, with several rectangular edifices placed at right-angles to one another, and surrounded by unkempt gardens and rows of palm-trees. Pot himself had briefly been a college-teacher at Tuol Sleng at the beginning of the 1960s, shortly before he had fled to the jungle from Sihanouk's police, and the rooms that had echoed with his readings of Rimbaud and Sade to his adoring students would now resound with the cacophony of screams generated by month-long torture sessions.

To run Tuol Sleng, Pot appointed a devoted Khmer Rouge acolyte, Kaing Kek Ieu. The insipid Ieu was chosen for his ability to write and keep detailed records (now a rare skill, after the wholesale purging of Cambodia's literate population) – Pot had decreed that, although writing had been summarily abolished in his revolutionary paradise, he would make an exception for Tuol Sleng, since he wanted to ascertain that all of the Cambodian intellectuals had been thoroughly interrogated and 'smashed' before their extermination. (Pot himself always refrained from writing anything himself during his years of power, and communicated all of his orders and edicts vocally.) For the post of chief interrogator at Tuol Sleng, Kaing Kek Ieu chose a tall, psychotic thug with a pock-marked face, Mam Nay, who had been a strong contender in Phnom Penh's pre-Pot criminal underworld and who towered over the midget-sized Kaing. In turn, Mam Nay then recruited all of the most cruel and unquestioning of his former associates, to act as his assistants at Tuol Sleng. Strangely, Kaing (or 'The Chief', as he was known) was to adroitly survive the entirety of Pot's years of murderous power, and later became a born-again Christian and United Nations aid-worker. He provided a cogent explanation for Pot's aberrant and mysterious rise to power, arguing that Pot had been the Antichrist. The irrefutable evidence was that Pot, like the Antichrist, had suddenly appeared out of the East with his braying hordes, and had instituted a state of seething chaos, in which he himself stood at the very centre, simultaneously both all-powerful and invisible. After receiving divine adulation from his subjects, Pot – like the Antichrist – had, together with his malevolent warriors, unleashed vast rivers of blood and lethal turmoil, had instituted the total fall of darkness upon the land, and had then mutated and abruptly vanished, leaving behind only a blackened, fire-seared wasteland strewn with millions of slaughtered carcasses.

The methods of torture devised by Pot for the Cambodian ex-intellectuals – and carried out by Mam Nay and his 'brothers' under the supervision of Kaing Kek Ieu – were not entirely sophisticated. What interested Pot above all was to extend the length of time to which his 'enemies' could be subjected to torture. In this, he was inspired by legendary accounts of the regime of torture instituted by his hero, the great leper-Emperor Jayavarman VII, who had insisted that captured spies, together with groups of prisoners acquired during his forces' rampages across South-East Asia, had to be kept alive and sensorially alert under torture for periods of two to three months, in order to appreciate the gravity of their crimes against the Angkor Empire. Jayavarman VII had ordered his scribes and scientists to invent the most intricate and agonizing means of torture ever inflicted, and an entire library had been meticulously compiled of these tortures.

Unfortunately for Pot, this unique library was no longer available to him – the colonial French had pillaged it in the mid-1920s from its place of hiding in one of the abandoned temples of Angkor Wat, and its contents had then been employed by the French neo-fascist colonial forces in their brutal interrogation and mass-torturing of North African captives during the Algerian War in the late 1950s. As a result, Pot's strategies of torture had to be mainly derived from those used by his other hero, Stalin, in the cellars of the Lubyanka in Moscow, with several added innovations suggested by his readings of Sade. But, whenever Pot passed on his detailed vocal instructions to Kaing Kek Ieu, who relayed them on to the dull-witted Mam Nay, who in turn delegated them to his moronic assistants, the intricate systems of torture assembled by Pot dissolved along the chain of command into the frenzied form of unsophisticated out-and-out assaults on the victim. As a result of these misfortunes, Pot's 'enemies' failed fully to receive the benefits of the long and rich history of human torture.

Each of the torture rooms at Tuol Sleng contained an object known as a 'bed of death' (although relatively few of the intellectuals actually died under the process of torture itself): a bare bed-frame to which each of the victims' limbs was tied with wire. Mam Nay's assistants would then use their arsenal of torture instruments at random, switching from whippings to bludgeonings of the sexual organs, removal of facial features with pliers and other sharp instruments, and the judicious application of electric prongs. Occasionally, they would apply the 'hot method' to their victims with blow-torches, but the scarcity of fuel resources in Pot's revolutionary eden meant that this was a 'special' treatment and a rarely-used luxury. Unleashing rats proved to be a less costly solution. The former intellectuals were kept in isolation in their cells for most of the days and nights, and a rota was instituted so that everyone would receive their due quota of torture on a regular basis. The obligation of keeping the ex-intellectuals alive for several months meant that they could only be tortured for short periods at a time. Nobody was given preferential treatment, and all of the temporary inhabitants of Tuol Sleng – male and female, young and old – were theoretically subject to the same regime of torture, subject to variance according to the arbitrary whims of Mam Nay's often-undisciplined assistants.

The necessity of keeping alive the former intelligentsia (many of whom were actually blameless shop-keepers or artisans, who had been corralled-in with the intellectuals in the confusion of the first days following Pot's victory, when the young Khmer Rouge cadres were haphazardly organizing the ex-city people's death-marches) over a period of several months was motivated by the requirement for them to have abundant time to confess their crimes before they were thoroughly 'smashed' by Pot's revolutionary will. Pot stipulated that Kaing Kek Ieu – who eventually had to recruit more and more assistants of his own for the purpose – had to transcribe every word spoken by his victims under torture, in order to gather 'proof' of the intellectuals' plans to betray the Khmer Rouge to their 'megacolonialist' enemies, which now principally comprised the USA, France, Britain and Vietnam. Kaing and his assistants meticulously took down the confessions, which often ran to hundreds of pages. Many of the confessions were addressed to Pot in person (or, more exactly, to the shadowy, nameless figure who controlled the Khmer Rouge, since Pot was still only rarely referred to or seen in public). The intellectuals – like the victims and former associates of Stalin – often believed that if they could sufficiently praise Pot's regime and point out to him the bizarre error which had led to their imprisonment and torture, he would certainly liberate them. Other intellectuals declined to confess their crimes and instead pointed out that Pot was a psychotic post-colonial pawn who had been pre-programmed by the French colonials to destroy the country after their own humiliated departure, in order to demonstrate how the French, by contrast, had 'protected' Cambodia and given it a high level of culture and refinement. In the end, Kaing Kek Ieu and his assistants grew tired of having to transcribe the verbose intellectuals' monologues, and received Pot's permission for the intellectuals to write down their own confessions in their cells, which they were eager to do. The masses of handwritten confessions, once typed, would be sent over to Pot's compound, where he relaxed in an armchair in the evenings after his revolutionary duties with a glass of his favourite 'Suntory' whiskey, impassively reading every last word of the confessions, while a small group of his sixteen-year-old Khmer Rouge cadres of both sexes would kneel in a line, taking turns to expertly fellate the 'Great Apparatus'.

Once the ex-intellectuals, smoothly progressing on Pot's conveyor-belt of death, had reached the stage of being 'smashed' (usually now minus most of their facial features, some of their intestines and the use of two or three limbs, as well as the power of speech), Kaing Kek Ieu would order them to be dispatched over to the Khmer Rouge execution squads who waited at one of the side-gates of Tuol Sleng in order to take the half-dead, blindfolded intellectuals away to the Choeung Ek death-fields of rich black mud. The removals usually happened at night. The unresisting intellectuals were then finished-off with arbitrary beatings of their addled skulls by metal clubs or, occasionally, when there was a backlog or surfeit to be cleared, by brief blasts of machine-gun fire. By the spring of Pot's Year Two (1977), the vast majority of the criminal intellectuals had been terminally 'sent to study'. The execution squads assigned to this duty rarely flinched in their work of extermination. The Khmer Rouge sixteen-year-old cadres of both sexes who had been born in 1961 proved to be even more uncompromised and devoted to the great vision of Pot than their predecessors who had been born in 1959 or 1960, and whom they would eventually be ordered to 'smash', as that older generation began to lose their pure revolutionary will. Outside Phnom Penh, piles of excess, still-blindfolded skulls and fractured bones soon started to accumulate and spill out of the black earth where they had been hapahazardly buried.

Before any of the fifteen thousand intellectuals had been 'smashed', Pot had ordered that each should be photographed at Tuol Sleng, moments before they entered the torture room. Kaing Kek Ieu had rounded up all of the surviving photographers who had been in business in Phnom Penh before the arrival of Pot's revolutionary forces; many of the photographers had already been worked to death or had vanished into oblivion in the peasant trenches of rural Cambodia, and others had to be pulled out from the death-marches which were still aimlessly crisscrossing the entire expanse of the country. The urban photographers had been used to satisfying a clientele who required a suitably cheerful photograph to be taken to celebrate a fortunate event such as a marriage or a success in business; their new assignment, with its terminal clientele, was the antithesis of that work. They were now the image-takers and mediators of death. One of the rooms at Tuol Sleng was converted into the photographers' studio, and they worked in relays to capture the images of all the faces – usually despondent and surly, but occasionally managing an ingratiating smile – of the imminently dead. Duplicates of the photographs were catalogued and stored in Kaing Kek Ieu's office. But the original photographs were painstakingly assembled together into a vast Book of Death, composed of 1,500 pages with ten photographs arranged on each page, and bound with a thick black leather cover. Once the last intellectual had been 'smashed', the Book of Death was completed, and Kaing presented it to Pot. The Book of Death then became the personal property of Pot. It was the one and only book created in Cambodia during Pot's years of power, and the one and only piece of personal property that was allowed to exist under his revolutionary regime. It remained with Pot until his own death, and he would finally be cremated with his Book of Death in his arms.

Pot himself occasionally made visits to Tuol Sleng in the spring of 1977, to gauge for himself how the work of extermination had been progressing. Only a few hundred of the most die-hard intellectuals (usually those of a post-structuralist persuasion) had still survived being 'smashed', and Pot began to castigate the staff of Tuol Sleng for their failure to fulfil their quotas of annihilation. The remaining ex-intellectuals would be summarily exterminated by the Khmer Rouge cadres over the next few weeks. As he walked around Tuol Sleng with the midget Kaing Kek Ieu and the oversized Mam Nay, Pot politely complained that they had not been working hard enough, and that they themselves were in danger of being 'sent to study'. Pot had read all of the confessions submitted for his attention by Kaing, but they had not succeeded in convincing him that he now had the means to protect his revolutionary state against potential incursions from the rampaging 'megacolonialists', and nor had the confessions been exhaustive enough to provide him with the means to extirpate all of his enemies,

whom he now began to refer to in his radio addresses as the 'microbes'. In his nightly broadcasts to his people, Pot commented, 'Enemies and wreckers attack and torment us... We will search for the microbes within ourselves... We will locate the repulsive microbes and they will be pushed out by our revolution. If we wait, if we are weak, the microbes will do real damage.' In order to isolate and destroy the 'microbes', Pot desperately needed more confessions, and it was now time for the Khmer Rouge themselves to provide them.

From the summer of 1977, the Khmer Rouge cadres began to arrest one another for counter-revolutionary crimes against the vision of Pot, and the cells at Tuol Sleng, recently vacated by their intellectual residents, began to fill up again. One of Pot's deputies, Son Sen, selected which traitors among the Khmer Rouge should be 'sent to study'. A few hundred peasants were also arrested and interrogated at Tuol Sleng, but their confessions were of such little interest to Pot – 'We criminally planted the rice... We criminally waited for the water-buffaloes to defecate to provide us with fertilizer...' – that he exonerated the entire peasantry of Cambodia for their transgressions, and allowed them to continue with their authentic work of complaining about bad harvests and beating the surviving '17 April' people under their supervision. At first, the Khmer Rouge revolutionaries from the provincial areas of Cambodia that adjoined the frontiers with Vietnam and Thailand bore the brunt of the arbitrary arrests ordered by Pot and Son Sen. From the resulting confessions, Pot was able to ascertain that there were rumblings from the Cambodia/Vietnam border about the possibility of an eventual Vietnamese invasion, motivated both by the historical precedents of Vietnam's regular incursions into Cambodia to confiscate its gem resources, and also by misgivings among the Communist leaders of Vietnam about Pot's unorthodox approach to revolutionary activity. With this information, Pot was now fully justified in his strategy of exacting an ever-higher rate of confessions, and he ordered all-out arrests of potential traitors and enemies within the Khmer Rouge ranks – all of his followers who could no longer demonstrate a pure level of utter subjugation to Pot's great project for Cambodia were instantly dispatched to Tuol Sleng. Soon, the death facility was bursting at the seams with new prisoners, all eager to confess, and a huge over-accumulation of victims and confessions jammed Tuol Sleng.

Next, Pot decided that the guards and interrogators of Tuol Sleng themselves were to blame for the criminally poor level of confession material, and he ordered the immediate 'smashing' of the pock-marked thug Mam Nay, who fervently provided the longest and most detailed confession yet produced at Tuol Sleng before being intensively tortured by his successor, and taking his due place in the now-saturated death-fields of skulls and bones. Then, all of Mam Nay's assistants (and their entire families) also had to be 'smashed', since their association with the criminal Mam had rendered them intractable 'enemies' of Pot's revolution. The rapid turnover of guards and interrogators at Tuol Sleng intensified over the summer of 1977, with Mam's successors also being summarily 'smashed' for exactly the same crime; the escalation of arrests, torturings and 'smashings' went on, while the interrogators at Tuol Sleng became younger and younger, and ever more attuned to the absence of compromise Pot demanded of them in their revolutionary duties. Pot constantly incited them to extract the lost fragments of information that would finally allow him to locate the lethal 'microbes' that were making his Cambodian revolution begin to disintegrate. Pot was kept frantically busy every night reading endless reams of monotonous confessions, and suffered a serious resurgence of his long-standing intestinal problems (the chefs who prepared Pot's meals at his compound now also came under suspicion, and after being denounced as 'wreckers', they and their entire families also found themselves abruptly facing a regime of blowtorches and electric prods at Tuol Sleng). But despite the constant necessity of replacing the interrogators and guards at Tuol Sleng, Pot was always prepared to spare the life of its incompetent midget commandant, Kaing Kek Ieu, whose allegiance to Pot was total.

Finally, Pot decided that many of his co-leaders and allies in the Khmer Rouge hierarchy, such as Keo Meas and Khek Penn, were now also insufficiently devoting themselves to his great vision, and might in the future attempt to usurp him or to ally themselves with his enemies – as a result, they too became his deadly enemies (along with all of their families and acquaintances), and found themselves arrested and dispatched for torture to Tuol Sleng. Some of these associates of Pot's were in their early fifties, as the 'Great Apparatus' himself now was, and had been his allies as far back as the early 1950s in Paris, since the long-gone nights of revolutionary meetings in the cafe in the rue Gît-le-Coeur. Pot demanded that Kaing Kek Ieu himself should supervise 'prolonged use of the hot method' for these special enemies, who were always astonished that their long-standing association with Pot counted for nothing in the face of his suspicions. Pot also ordered some of his most resolute supporters who were based in other countries, especially France and Vietnam, to return immediately to Phnom Penh to 'participate more closely in the revolution'; on arrival in Phnom Penh, the cars sent to collect them and take them for their urgent meetings with 'Brother Number One' would head instead for the southern suburbs, and Pot's old companions would soon find themselves tightly ligatured to a bare bed-frame, face-to-face with a group of glowering sixteen-year-olds wielding blowtorches and demanding information on the whereabouts of the 'microbes'. Most of these special victims of Pot's wrath were intensively tortured to death, rather than being taken away to be finished-off at the Choeung Ek killing-zone; their ravaged carcasses were then simply thrown into a pit in the grounds of Tuol Sleng. After Pot's radical purge of his former allies, control over the Khmer Rouge forces shrank to only four participants besides the supreme leader, Pot: Ieng Sary, Son Sen, Nuon Chea and Ta Mok – all of them fanatical supporters of Pot's revolution.

By the end of September 1977, the essential work of Death Facility S-21 at Tuol Sleng was over, and Pot had 'smashed' all of the enemies he could think of for the time being. The criminal ex-intelligentsia had now been entirely massacred; the interrogators and torturers who had failed to thoroughly extract confessions from the intellectuals had also now been exterminated, together with their successors and their successors' successors (and all of their entire families). In addition, Pot had successfully rid himself of all of his allies who might, at some point in the future, have even contemplated resisting his revolutionary vision for Cambodia. And he had obliterated those traitors who had been consorting with 'megacolonialists' in the reactionary hotbeds of France and Vietnam. Meanwhile, in the death-zones outside Phnom Penh and the other cities of Cambodia (where subsidiary variants of Tuol Sleng had also been operating at full-tilt), the black earth disgorged thousands upon thousands of shattered skulls and bones, packed so tightly into the ground that the resulting pressure forced them to crack open the surface of the hot earth and emerge into the open air. The Khmer Rouge sixteen-year-old revolutionary cadres, now short of employment after the all-out decimation of Pot's enemies had been accomplished, began to arrange the individual skulls into great collective pyramids of death, as monuments to Pot's annihilatory will and his glorious triumph in extirpating the treacherous 'microbes' that had plagued the first years of his revolution. Pot himself was now planning the next stage of that revolution: the alliance of his murderous totalitarian vision to the integrally sexual dimensions of revolutionary power. But first, he planned to make a trip outside Cambodia, where there would be a suitably mediatized stage for him to reveal himself to the whole world.

POL POT'S YEAR ZERO SEX SLAVE SYSTEM

Pot's grand tour of China and North Korea in September and October 1977 served to crystallize his new status as the great philosopher of freedom gained through totalitarian sexual subjugation and death, and also allowed him the valuable opportunity to expound his great vision for the future of Cambodia to the media. When he arrived in Beijing on 28 September, Pot was treated as a visiting deity: as his limousine rolled into the city centre from the airport, millions of children energetically waved the black flag of Democratic Kampuchea and shouted greetings to their visitor, who was hidden-away behind smoked, bullet-proof glass. Pot was immediately given a lavish banquet, and offered the sexual services of as many thirteen-year-old virgins as he might wish (Communist China's revolutionary leader, Mao Tse-tung, who had finally expired in the previous year, had been notorious for his well-documented sexual demands on his adolescent cadres, but preferred to be serviced by an even younger generation than Pot, especially exacting revolutionary sexual duties from eager eleven-year-old party-activists). Pot met the new leaders of China, who had been engaged in a murderous, all-out power struggle with one another since the death of their 'Great Pilot': the sly Deng Xiaoping, who would eventually seize power (and would gratuitously butcher his people in Tienanmen Square in an act of atrocity almost on a par with Pot), incessantly flattered and fawned over Pot, suggesting that he was now the sole hope for authentic revolutionary action in South-East Asia. (His real motivation for inviting Pot to China and ostentatiously entertaining him was actually to provoke and taunt the Vietnamese Communists, who were allied to China's rivals, the Soviet Union.) Although television was outlawed in Pot's visionary eden, he magnanimously agreed to two television interviews. In the first, on 29 September, transmitted live on China's one state channel, he announced his true identity as 'Pol Pot', explaining that it had been necessary in the first two years of his regime for him to be a nameless but beneficent and omniscient presence, ably guiding his people through the chaos left behind by Sihanouk. In his second interview, for the 'TV Transjug' channel of Yugoslavia (whose affable dictator, Tito, had allied himself with the Chinese after a bitter feud with the Soviet Union), Pot commented that 'We have built a new generation of intellectuals' and elucidated his great plan for Cambodia, explaining that 'Our national revolution has taken radical steps to root out traitors, microbes and enemies. We have made great strides, in the face of our megacolonialist enemies – and we are only just beginning!'. The interview for Yugoslavian television, which the urbane and still-handsome Pot conducted without ever losing his beaming, self-deprecating smile, impressed many of the then-emerging Serbian nationalist leaders, such as the poet Radovan Karadzic, who regarded it as a seminal influence on his own future genocidal work in Bosnia. The interview, given in Pot's fluent French and subtitled in Serbo-Croat, was also screened on French television, where it made a deep impression on the Maoist literary intellectuals, such as Philippe Sollers, who were then at the zenith of their short-lived popularity. The Chinese marked Pot's departure with even more excessive celebrations than his arrival, relieved that the amiable but clearly-lunatic totalitarian was now exiting. On his way back to the airport, the millions of corralled schoolchildren appeared again, this time with banners inscribed 'Thank You For Your Visit, Adorable Pot'.

From China, Pot and his entourage flew on to the isolated Stalinist-style state of North Korea, where the country's addled despot, Kim Il Sung, was waiting for him. Again, Pot was revered as a revolutionary god, and provided another television interview in which he pointed out that only he, Stalin and (to be polite to his host) Kim Il Sung possessed the absolute will required to 'extirpate all microbes within the Revolutionary Organization'. The only sour note was that the senile Kim Il Sung mistakenly assumed that, since Pot had not mercilessly culled the regal fop Sihanouk (who was still locked in his palace, awaiting in terror the unknown moment of his death), he must still be allied to the princely sophisticate in some way, and gave Pot a barrel of football-sized apples to take back with him as a present for the consumerist Sihanouk. As a result, Pot seethed angrily all the way back to Phnom Penh. However, he was also returning from his trip with a present that was much more to his liking: a film, entitled *Democratic Kampuchea Leaps Forward!*, that had been made by the Chinese as a special gift for him; a group of Chinese film-makers had toured Cambodia in the preceding months, shooting images of grinning peasants and grim-faced Khmer Rouge cadres, and carefully avoiding the omnipresent scenes of mass-carnage. New sequences showing Pot's reception in Beijing had been hurriedly edited into the footage. Unfortunately, there was now no cinema in Phnom Penh in which to show Pot's film, since his revolutionary forces had summarily burned down the city's one cinema (which had currently been showing *Emmanuelle* for the twentieth month in a row) on 17 April 1975. Pot immediately ordered the construction of a Stalinist 'palace of culture' in the depopulated city, where the film was to be screened daily to an empty hall. A one-off screening was also arranged in order to goad Sihanouk, who looked enviously at the filmed scenes of the well-attired Pot being served forty-course dinners in lavish banquet halls full of fashionable-looking dignitaries, and commented: 'It is all far more magnificent than anything I have ever received myself.'

On his return to Cambodia, Pot now revealed himself to his people as 'Pol Pot' in a special radio broadcast – his few surviving sisters were astonished to learn that their genial younger brother, Sar, whom they had once initiated into the eleven profound secrets of sexual self-annulment, was in fact the all-powerful 'Great Apparatus', now engaged in assiduously propelling his country into a terminally brutal state of chaos and decimating implosion. Most of the peasantry and surviving city-people were oblivious to the revelation that the insignificant minor aristocrat Saloth Sar had turned out to be 'Brother Number One', Pol Pot, while his revolutionary cadres revered him as intensively as ever. But for Pot himself, this was the crucial moment in his long career as a genocidal mass-murderer. He had now taken public responsibility for his revolutionary acts, rather than remaining hidden in the bloody miasma of induced terror and dense mystery which he had cultivated in his first years of power. At the end of 1977, Pot began to put into operation his project for a Year Zero Sex Slave System, whose origins he adroitly backdated to the glorious moment of his revolutionary victory on 17 April 1975. This project was to be Pot's supreme and last obsession. Until the discovery, four years after Pot's death, of the cryptic notes made in secret by his associates in power at their monthly meetings, little was known of Pot's grand plan to institute a systematic regime of revolutionary sexual annihilation; even now, this lost agenda of Pot's ambitious final project for Cambodia has to be pieced together from half-destroyed fragments. Although Pot despised the crass 'cult of personality' which he associated with Sihanouk and foreign revolutionary leaders such as the moribund Mao, he was determined to espouse a magisterial public image that would fully transmit his twin totalitarian compulsions with controlling all death and all sex: Pot would now lead his people from a deific, malevolent position of sexual obliteration coupled with extreme, lethal power.

The first stage in Pot's plan was easily accomplished. In the final months of 1977, he instituted the end of the family. All of the Cambodian peasantry would now be expelled from their dung-encrusted hovels, and re-housed as sexual collectives in the plywood bunkers that had previously accommodated the massacred '17 April' people. All marriages were instantly dissolved, and all sexual acts between couples formally prohibited (although incest was vigorously encouraged). The collective revolutionary sexual future of Cambodia required that, as a first step, the entire conception of sex itself had to be returned to zero. The 'old society' needed to be mercilessly extirpated and consigned to the oblivion of history. Pot began testing out his plan in experimental zones of the country, where it transpired that the dull-witted peasantry were expressing reservations about Pot's grand project. His revolutionary sixteen-year-old Khmer Rouge cadres were soon sent to decapitate the reactionary peasant-criminals and strike mass-terror into the rest of the peasantry. Once the sexual participants were surrounded with a litter of severed heads, they were more receptive to Pot's visionary scheme. He had learned from his visit to China that the peasantry there were expected to regularly undertake 'storming attacks' on their crops, which involved the frenetic harvesting of entire fields in the space of seconds. He now demanded that 'sexual storming attacks' should be instituted right across Cambodia, so that the maximum number of sexual acts (preferably of an incestuous, bestial or deviant form) could be accomplished, in order to whip the entire country up into a sensorially vertiginous state of revolutionary overkill.

An integral part of Pot's great scheme was to ally his demands for higher productivity in sex with his simultaneous demands for a far greater output of excrement on the part of his population. Again, 'storming attacks' were the answer. At the end of 1977, having gauged the total production of excrement in Cambodia by cross-referencing reports from sewerage engineers working in the country's fast-crumbling drainage system with estimates of the total amount of excrement being used by the peasantry to grow crops in the fields, Pot came to the devastating conclusion that Cambodia was operating at a sub-quota ratio in the domain of excrement. This was certainly in large part the result of infiltration and sabotage on the part of the 'megacolonialist' enemies of Cambodia. But some of the blame also rested with Pot's subjects themselves. He immediately issued a revolutionary edict: 'Production of natural human fertilizer must rise from 5.6 million tons in Year Two [1977] to 8.9 million tons in Year Five [1980]: all Democratic Kampucheans who fail to produce their required quota will be sent to study.' It was clear that the necessary 'great leap forward' in excrement production would require a vast effort of revolutionary will on the part of Pot's population. The threatened peasantry, already under orders to vastly increase the number of arbitrary sexual acts they performed in the course of their working day, were now compelled to eat as much roughage, weeds and dirt as they could lay their hands on, in order to attempt to fulfil their quota and – if possible – become revolutionary super-quota workers in the all-important sphere of excrement. Pot and his associate Son Sen calculated that the quantitative differentials between the production of excrement and of sexual fluids needed to be radically adjusted, in order that the population could work all-out on their twin revolutionary duties. Relentless anal sex was one solution, and the sodden fields of Cambodia soon teemed with masses of peasants buggering one another, scanned by the watchful eyes of the gun-toting Khmer Rouge cadres. Under the burning sun of Cambodia, the rural population started to sink beneath great orgasmic expulsions of excrement, semen and skull-encrusted liquefied mud.

At the beginning of 1978 – which was to prove to be his final year of power – Pot assembled all of his innovations for the sexual future of Cambodia into the form of an all-encompassing, secret Five-Year-Plan: any failure on the part of the population to deliver the required results would mean immediate extermination. The devastating sensorial momentum he had imparted to Cambodia now had to be sustained and exacerbated at all cost. An intensive corporeal revolution needed to be allied and then seamlessly merged with the totalitarian frenzy of mass-murdering and carnage which he had already succeeded in generating. But the incandescent sexual experimentation instituted by Pot was already beginning to fade. The terrible obstacle to the realization of Pot's scheme was that he had already thoroughly eliminated a large percentage of Cambodia's population (between two-and-a-half and three million: nobody was counting the exact figure any longer, since anyone capable of counting was liable for execution), and the remaining peasantry were now reeling with exhaustion at the demands exacted upon them to produce more crops, to engender a vast sexual and excremental furore, and to commit themselves utterly to Pot's revolutionary vision. Only the Khmer Rouge cadres themselves could be depended upon to rigorously follow the edicts of Pot; but even the most ruthlessly pure sixteen-year-old revolutionaries were now beginning to falter. Pot had instilled in them the vision that all authentic revolutionary acts involved the arbitrary subjugation, massacre and violation of enemies and traitors – and now there was only a scattering of criminals still left to kill, as Pot determinedly unearthed the remaining 'microbes' among his former associates. Unless Pot elected to 'smash' the five million members of the Cambodian peasantry itself (in which case there would simply be nobody left alive in the slaughtered and storm-whipped expanse of Cambodia at all, apart from Pot himself and his Khmer Rouge die-hards), their merciless revolutionary will was in danger.

Pot had decided that he would detonate and demolish the massive Angkor Wat imperial complex of temples which Jayavarman VII had completed (by developing existing constructions from the reigns of previous emperors) in the twelfth century; in its place, Pot would build an equally vast monument to mark his revolutionary sexual 'leap forward' for Cambodia. Pot himself had now superseded his first hero, the leper-Emperor, both in his capacity to inflict supreme cruelty (enhanced in Pot's case by his willingness to exact massacres upon his own people, while Jayavarman VII had principally confined himself to torturing and decimating the populations of other countries or empires whom he had encountered on his amok invasions around the South-East Asian landmass), and also in his relentless will for collective sexual innovation. Some of Pot's acolytes among the Khmer Rouge leadership, including the now-unemployed midget-commandant of Tuol Sleng, Kaing Kek Ieu, had an alternative plan for Angkor Wat, and secretly planned to build a gigantic, Stalin-style concrete figure of Pot himself on the demolished site, pointing his finger in wrath towards his 'megacolonialist' enemies, and flanked by his revolutionary cadre clutching their massed weaponry. However, Pot's acolytes soon realised that such a crass demonstration would have been distasteful to the often self-effacing and evasive Pot. As a first step in his plan for Angkor Wat, Pot sent some of his Khmer Rouge followers to the site, and they gradually succeeded in destroying much of the complex by using the gigantic statues of the faces of gorgeous courtesans for arbitrary target-practice, and by shooting mortars into its temples (killing many of the monks who were taking refuge there). But it soon became clear that the complex had been too solidly-constructed by Jayavarman VII ever to be fully dismantled. Pot's only solution was to reinvent Angkor Wat as the first Khmer Rouge tourist destination, and he invited his Chinese and North Korean allies to send 'revolutionary tourists' to view his work-in-progress of demolition at Angkor Wat. In the end, Pot had to entirely abandon this element of his grand plan, although the Khmer Rouge would continue to inhabit the Angkor Wat complex as one of their northern military bastions after the fall of Pot, planting many thousands of landmines around it.

Pot's final variant in his Sade-inspired projects for the revolutionary sexual upheaval of Cambodia was his plan to instigate a country-wide sex slave system, to be administered and controlled only by the most authentic of the peasants and the most uncompromised of the Khmer Rouge cadres. The project would operate along the same tried-and-tested model as the previous mass-obliteration through overwork and beatings of the 'April 17' people, with each 'master' of a subjugated collective of slaves having the authority to order and oversee as many acts of sexual furore and outright atrocity as might be desired; these acts would oscillate between ordering vast, communal sessions of sodomy (lasting for months on end without respite), and the abrupt massacring – on the master's arbitrary caprice – of the entire collective of slaves. In such a system, revolutionary sexual ecstasy would be fired to white-hot furnace-levels via ever-greater intensities of annihilation and orgasmic frenzies. But once again, Pot failed either to locate either the quantity of slaves necessary to generate such sensory upheavals, and lacked too the peasants and cadres with the degree of revolutionary determination necessary to oversee such experiments. Pot's own headlong power-excesses had finally brought his revolutionary project for the allied sexual and totalitarian transformations of Cambodia to a grinding halt. He had simply sent too many of his people to study.

As a result of the mass-depopulation and generalized sexual exhaustion of Cambodia, Pot had to work with what he had left in his final year of power. Faced with his addled, fatigued peasantry, and the now-crumbling revolutionary will of his Khmer Rouge cadre, he turned his focus instead to the form of Cambodia itself – with its depopulated cities, their boulevards still strewn with the now-skeletal remains of the inhabitants who had been summarily executed on 17 April 1975; with its cities' outlying, over-packed slaughter-zones, such as Choeung Ek, where endless swathes of blind-folded skulls and broken bones now forced their way out of the black earth; and with its rural areas, where the vast burial pits of the overworked ex-urban inhabitants had been only nonchalantly covered-over by their peasant tormentors. Cambodia itself now comprised one immense anatomical violation – a black void of cruelty, scarred by countless acts of atrocity, still smouldering noxiously with the residues of US napalm and bacteriological weaponry, and held together only by the accumulation of its endless quantities of shattered skulls. The very identity of Cambodia itself was encompassed by the inextricably-entwined twin forms of Pot's murderous and sexual compulsions. Cambodia now held the prescient traces of the annihilation of the human race itself, in the final revolution that would be the definitive stage of Pot's planned work. But whatever ultimate, worldwide carnage might be generated from the terminal, near-apocalyptic zone of human negation that Pot had created for Cambodia, it was certain that Pot himself would survive as the dominant figure within that corroded landscape, still retaining his status as 'Brother Number One' to the end.

THE BLACK POWER OF POL POT'S LAST YEAR

During his final year of total power over Cambodia, Pot's isolation and increasing paranoia in his fortified compound within the palace complex in Phnom Penh led him to envisage schemes of an extreme and bizarre nature, alongside which his grand plan for the mass sexual subjugation and self-obliteration of his people appears eminently restrained and mundane. Guarded by his fierce cannibalistic tribesmen, who machine-gunned, decapitated and then ingested anyone foolish enough to approach Pot's compound, the 'Great Apparatus' spent the last months of his revolutionary regime developing plans to export his genocidal product to the outside world. He began to issue taunts in his radio broadcasts to the Vietnamese Communists, calling them 'lily-livered second-rate revolutionaries' and inciting them to put into practice a 'vision' for Vietnam that would match his own decimating innovations. However, despite his growing isolation (only Pot's four chief acolytes in the Khmer Rouge leadership now had close contact with him), Pot's demeanour remained affable and suave at all times. Even his orders to commit the most eviscerating of tortures and the most arbitrary of atrocities were articulated with supreme politeness, and he always instructed his executioners to transmit the deepest of apologies for disturbing his victims before they were skinned alive and then blow-torched into formless masses of lacerated carbon. During his last months of power *in extremis*, the well-groomed Pot coupled an ever-charming smile with his obsessional distrust of his obsequious associates (an obsession that was fully justified) and with his ever-expanding sense of the conspiracies being hatched against his revolution, all of which merited the most brutal of 'smashings'.

In the spring of 1978, Pot realised with horror that he had still not massacred Cambodia's large population of self-flagellating monks; although the owners of the country's monasteries had been culled, he had neglected the monks themselves up until now because of his preoccupation with his more-urgent revolutionary duties. Around three hundred thousand monks were still hiding fearfully in their temples and monasteries, or in the forests or fields around them, hoping that Pot had forgotten all about them or that – because he himself had once been destined to lead a monk's austere life of covert buggery and whippings, before he had left for Paris – Pot had decided to spare them from his revolutionary wrath. The only fatalities among them had been those killed by accident, such as the monks sheltering in the Angkor Wat temples who had been blown apart by mortar fire during Pot's attempts to demolish the vast complex. Pot now quickly dispatched the most uncompromised of his Khmer Rouge followers and bodyguards to burn and destroy the monasteries and to round-up the monks, who were whipped along into fields of bone-encrusted black earth, and then clubbed and decapitated in groups. The debauched monasteries had become immensely wealthy institutions over the previous centuries, since they preyed on the gullible peasantry for donations, and Pot's abrupt devastation of them led to the accretion of vast wealth for the Khmer Rouge coffers; but, since money was rigorously outlawed in Pot's revolutionary eden, all of the lavish hoards of gold coins had to be buried in a big hole in the ground, along with the shattered and often-headless bodies of the monks themselves. The monks' crumpled skulls were set aside to be added to the mountainous cranial accumulations that marked the peripheries of Pot's depopulated cities, often assembled into pyramidal constructions by those of Pot's sixteen-year-old cadres who were not actively engaged in the culling of the counter-revolutionary religious 'wreckers'. The summary dispatching of the dissolute monks into the bloody void would earn Pot a high ranking in the Buddha's cosmology for services rendered to oblivion and nirvana, thereby ensuring him immediate entry into the Shining Land on his own demise.

Once the monasteries had been emptied, Pot toured Cambodia for the last time, riding in a cavalcade of black Zil limousines with his entourage of machine-gun toting bodyguards. Although the monks had been thoroughly purged, it became apparent that many of the centuries-old monasteries had only been damaged and were still standing; these signs of negligence on the part of his most trusted revolutionary cadres, some of whom were now starting to entertain their first doubts about the omniscience of Pot's great plans for Cambodia, indicated the slowly-accumulating disintegration of his regime. Pot, riled by every failure of his acolytes to carry through his vision, continued to massacre his allies, thereby adding to his already-maximal power. By culling his allies, Pot created power itself, since the pure revolutionary determination of those arbitrarily-slaughtered allies was transferred intact to Pot himself. At the same time, Pot continued to despise the crass manifestations of power, still refusing to have himself idolized as a lethal god in the way that Stalin had. Instead, he attempted with increasing desperation to maintain the aura of deadly mystery and self-effacement that had given the first years of his regime their unadulterated murderous strength. But, as Pot travelled through Cambodia, the entire blackened and firescorched landscape exuded only its emptiness of all human traces, with the surviving peasants hiding away in ditches or temporarily burying themselves under mud, and the waterlogged black earth disgorging endless masses of skulls.

On his tour of the Cambodian provinces, Pot regularly delivered speeches to his young revolutionary cadres at their training centres and outposts. At first, the appreciative cadres were impressed by the suave Pot's hypnotic delivery and by his ability to communicate his great projects to them in a modest and unassuming way, always beaming his warm, appealing smile at them and appearing to speak to each of them individually. But the relentless momentum of Pot's great vision meant that he had so much to impart to his followers that the speeches went on and on, regularly extending over five hours. Occasionally, when Pot – who never spoke from notes, since writing had been abolished – was carried away by his revolutionary exhilaration, he could speak for even longer; in the town on Kompong Speu on 23 April 1978, he began a speech that continued without a break for forty-eight hours. Nobody was allowed to leave or even to lose concentration for a single moment of Pot's diatribes, which revolved around the absolute necessity of extirpating 'microbes', of conducting 'storming attacks' of various kinds, and – increasingly – of execrating and cursing the counter-revolutionary hordes of Communist Vietnam. Like the Emperor Caligula, who decreed that every member of the audiences of the great spectacles of slaughter which he choreographed in the Roman Arena should compulsorily participate in the entire event – and that anyone attempting to leave would forfeit their life on the receiving end of a ravening lion's maw – Pot too exacted utter subservience to his revolutionary tirades. Any slackers were immediately 'sent to study'. After Pot's motorcade had driven off, the relieved cadres would collapse on the ground in exhaustion. Pot's radio-broadcasts, too, had been expanding to ever-greater levels of volubility over the previous six months: on 27 September 1977, he had given a five-hour speech which rapidly came to appear as a model of taciturn concision. The entirety of Radio Phnom Penh's output soon consisted of live broadcasts by Pot or else pre-recorded and repeated transmissions. The voice of Pot saturated the ether of Cambodia, though his listeners were now fewer and fewer.

In his final months of power, Pot often referred in his broadcasts to his own head as being like a pineapple. He possessed 'as many eyes as a pineapple' and was able to hover vigilantly over the heads of his population, penetrating their thoughts and actions, in order to ensure that they were engaged in revolutionary duties without respite for twenty-four hours each day. Even the few hours of sleep his people were permitted each night had to be devoted to the formulation of revolutionary resolve. The 'Great Pineapple' possessed an infinite capacity of visual surveillance, and out of that surveillance directly emerged the potential horror which the 'pineapple' had the benevolent capacity to exact, if it so wished – falling from space and battering its enemies' heads to the most unrecognisable pulp. Banana trees and sugarcanes, too, were sources of Pot's endless poetic metaphors for the unrelenting and unbreakable will with which he would decimate the 'megacolonialist' hordes that would soon be gathering at Cambodia's borders, but which could be repulsed effortlessly because of the pure ferocity of his revolutionary power. The now-starving peasantry of Cambodia, exhausted and malnourished after the pitifully poor harvests of Pot's years in power (the yields of which, in any case, were immediately confiscated by the Khmer Rouge cadres), listened to the broadcasts in order at least to hear the saliva-inducing litany of edible items to which Pot compared his indestructible regime.

Although he always spurned the idea of a 'personality cult' for himself, Pot grudgingly allowed the mass-production of shoddy concrete busts of his head and shoulders to be made during the final year of his regime. His old acolyte, the midget-commandant of Tuol Sleng, Kaing Kek Ieu, had persuaded him that this would be an efficient means to channel the terrified adulation of his population into ever-greater manifestations of neurally-exploded subjugation. Kaing supervised the experimental casting of the concrete busts by a group of seven artisans whom he had specially set aside from the slaughter-assigned inhabitants of his Death Facility (these were the only survivors of Tuol Sleng). The casting took place in a workshop in the grounds of Tuol Sleng, which was now operating at a criminally 'sub-quota' rate because of the dearth of suitable victims left to be 'smashed'. The incorrigible Kaing – desperate to appear useful to Pot so as to avoid being 'smashed' himself and thereby survive Pot's now-crumbling regime (which he succeeded in doing) – was still planning large-scale public works, such as four-hundred-metre high statues of the 'Great Apparatus', even vaster in scale than the one he had envisaged for the vacated site of Angkor Wat. The only obstacles to the homicidal midget's schemes were that there now remained virtually no supplies of construction materials in Cambodia, and certainly no architects or builders able to erect the grandiose edifices. And when the refined Pot himself viewed the crass concrete busts and plans for monuments, he abruptly ordered them to be broken and burned, and returned to his compound in a disconsolate fury.

The great tragedy of Pot's revolutionary eden was that it was malfunctioning through a lack of suitable enemies to decimate. While Pot himself demanded ever-greater levels of carnage, his projects were thwarted and blocked by the unavailability of candidates to pass through his death facilities and annihilation zones. With the intellectuals comprehensively 'smashed', the city-dwellers worked to death or clubbed into oblivion by malicious peasants, the monks slaughtered and even large swathes of his own Khmer Rouge followers mercilessly culled and purged, Cambodia now presented few opportunities for a truly ambitious genocidal tyrant. Pot sank into deeper despair at his intractable position. The only solution was that of expansion into new territories, and Pot renewed his nationalistic barrages of invective against Vietnam, along with Thailand and Japan; he warned his die-hard Khmer Rouge followers that he was going to instigate a new phase in their revolution, which would eventually involve a murderous rampage across South-East Asia (and beyond) that would be worthy of his hero's Jayavarman VII's own twelfth-century headlong invasions of mass-pillage and subjugation. Pot now also reactivated Tuol Sleng for the last time, channelling in more and more of the uncompromised Khmer Rouge revolutionaries who – through Pot's caprices – were transformed overnight into treacherous supporters of the threatening 'megacolonialists'. Over six thousand baffled cadres found themselves being interrogated about their status as 'microbes' at Tuol Sleng, then tortured, 'smashed' and nonchalantly butchered, over the final months of 1978; Kaing Kek Ieu was back in business. A dense mist of blood rose upwards into the sky from the Death Facility. The generalized bloodbath then widened and intensified out of all control: hundreds of thousands of other cadres, in the eastern and northern provinces of Cambodia, were simply slaughtered at their bases (whether they were under suspicion of treachery or not), together with all of their families and acquaintances. Leading figures in the upper echelons of the Khmer Rouge, such as Vorn Vet and Muo Sambath, were also ruthlessly exterminated in the escalating chaos of Pot's final months.

Pot remained in an affable mood throughout the terminal turmoil of his revolution. His leading acolytes, Son Sen and Ta Mok, visited his compound regularly to report on the progress of the massacres at Tuol Sleng and in the provinces, while Pot smiled amiably, relaxing in an armchair and taking sips of his favourite 'Suntory' whisky. He calmly ordered his acolytes to 'intensify the revolution' until it could develop the genocidal impetus necessary to burst over the frontiers of Cambodia itself and engulf the entire population of East Asia, thereby also terrifying the 'megacolonialists' of the USA, France and Britain, causing their own governments to collapse and their populations to self-implode in great urban massacres that would leave behind only cursed and smouldering tracts of depopulated, void territory. However, outside Pot's own personal pavilion, his compound was in uproar, simmering under pressure as rumours swept Phnom Penh that the Vietnamese were finally contemplating putting an end to Pot's regime. The cannibalistic tribesmen started to mutiny, threatening to abandon Phnom Penh and head back to their remote home regions in the north-east of the country. The compound increasingly resembled Pot's jungle headquarters of the early 1970s, with piles of severed heads marking its frontiers, while insanely-jabbering guards fired off salvoes of rockets and machine-gun blasts into the night sky. Pot remained calm, and decided that this was the appropriate moment to invite a few distinguished visitors from outside the country to come and survey the impressive results of his great work.

Pot's first visitor, at the beginning of December, was the Romanian dictator Nicolae Ceaucescu, who flew into Phnom Penh with an entourage of two hundred acolytes and liked what he saw. Ceaucescu himself had been suppressing and massacring his dissidents (though on a much smaller scale, and for genuine acts of opposition towards his regime) for twenty years, while defending Romania against the colonial intentions of the Soviet Union to incorporate it into its vast Empire. Ceaucescu's only ally besides Cambodia and North Korea was Britain, and on his state visits to London he regularly demanded a lavish dinner at Buckingham Palace with Queen Elizabeth II, distracting her attention by haranguing her about the evils of the Soviet Union while his wife, Elena, pocketed the silverware. Pot gave Ceaucescu a tour of the increasingly lawless countryside around the empty capital, showing him the comprehensively subjugated peasants (who resembled Ceaucescu's own) and the mass-extermination sites of those he had 'sent to study'. Ceaucescu's own schemes for Romania constituted a far more inept and lazily-pursued counterpart to Pot's great vision, but, before leaving in mid-December, the elderly tyrant gave a piece of fatherly advice to Pot, advising him to build an immense and sumptuous new palace in Phnom Penh, equipped with a balcony from which he could receive the adulation of his people, and with a helicopter take-off pad on the roof for a quick getaway if necessary. (Ceaucescu's own regime was to come to a sudden end exactly a decade later, when he was interrupted in mid-harangue on his palace balcony by his enraged population; even though Ceaucescu and his wife managed to make their expected helicopter getaway, they were tracked down by their former acolytes and summarily pumped with bullets on 25 December 1989, while Elena screamed at her executioners: 'You motherfuckers!').

Later in December, the Scottish pro-Pot journalist Malcolm Caldwell arrived in Phnom Penh at Pot's invitation, ready to write a series of adulatory articles for the international media in which Pot's regime would be lauded as possessing the greatest revolutionary will and the most courageous anti-colonial zeal in the whole of East Asia. On 23 December, Pot – who had now finally ditched his black pyjama-suits, and was wearing an elegant silver silk outfit – received Caldwell for an interview in which he explained the importance of removing microbes and outlined his future plans for the development of Cambodia. However, Caldwell's over-enthusiastic litany of servile praise soon became exasperating for the diffident and self-effacing Pot, and after the interview, he ordered that the obsequious Caldwell needed to be covertly executed for the crime of excess sycophancy. Demonstrations of boundless servitude merited only death in Pot's Cambodia. That night, a group of assassins broke into Caldwell's room in a guest-house alongside Pot's compound and arbitrarily slaughtered the bemused Scot while he was writing up his interview notes in glowing praise of Pot. In order to continue the success of his 'opening-up' of Cambodia to the outside world, Pot had also invited several leading French literary intellectuals to visit him at the end of December, including the writer Philippe Sollers, who had transferred his previous adulation for the now-deceased Mao to Pot. Many of the French intellectuals of the moment revered Pot, and Sollers in particular viewed him as the epitome of his own revolutionary aspirations. Pot had already decided that Sollers – clearly as fawning and servile as Caldwell – would be destined for the same fate as the culled Scot, and had already instructed that Sollers be dispatched straight from the airport to Tuol Sleng, to endure several months of torture with 'prolonged use of the hot method' before being mercilessly 'smashed' for his crimes. However, on the day before the unsuspecting Sollers was due to leave Paris for Phnom Penh, his visit was suddenly cancelled – the Vietnamese had just invaded Pot's revolutionary eden, and were rampaging at full-tilt towards Phnom Penh.

Pot's undoing had been his gratuitous taunting of the Vietnamese as 'second-class revolutionaries' – a theme he had elaborated on at interminable length during his radio broadcasts of December 1978. The Vietnamese Communist leadership had tolerated Pot and his excesses, which they knew about from the few fortunate exiles who had managed to cross the frontier into Vietnam and had reported on Pot's four-year-long frenzy of extermination. But, because of the delicate power-balance they were involved in (the Vietnamese were allied to the Soviet Union, while Pot's regime still had nominal ties to China from Pot's visit there in 1977), they had refrained from taking action. But Pot's insults finally pushed them over the edge. The Vietnamese army was still a highly-disciplined and expert force from its comprehensive victory over the USA in 1975, and on 25 December 1978 (at the very end of Year Three of Pot's regime) it swiftly tore through the enthusiastic attempts by Pot's sixteen-year-old revolutionary cadres to defend the Cambodian frontier. Once they had used up all of their bullets, Pot's uncompromised young revolutionaries ran in gangs directly at the Vietnamese army's hail of sub-machine gun fire, intending to throttle the invaders with their bare hands. A hundred thousand Vietnamese faced an equal number of Khmer Rouge (if Pot had not gratuitously exterminated over two hundred thousand of his own followers earlier in the year, the Vietnamese would have been outnumbered by three to one), and the superiority of the Vietnamese forces enabled them to sweep across the east of the country, reducing the Khmer Rouge forces to around ten thousand survivors by 1 January 1979, when the invaders neared Phnom Penh. A number of fleeing Khmer Rouge cadres in the east and south of the country were also bloodily dismembered and then violated in reprisals conducted by the peasants whom they had systematically subjugated and forcibly enrolled in Pot's revolutionary schemes, although other elements of the peasantry, especially in the north-west of the country, remained loyal to Pot.

By 2 January, mortars were exploding all around Pot's compound, though the mood of the 'Great Apparatus' remained positive, and he was nonchalant about the imminent danger. The Khmer Rouge troops defending Phnom Penh gave way (many of them engulfed and suffocated by the sodden, bone-encrusted mud which had been pounded into liquefaction by the Vietnamese artillery) and the Vietnamese forces finally came within sight of the immense pyramids of shattered skulls that marked the edge of the city. Pot then decided that it was time for him to receive a visit from the regal fop Sihanouk, who had been barricaded in his palace for almost four years, awaiting the unknown moment of death. Sihanouk fully expected Pot to exterminate him, but Pot greeted him on the steps of his pavilion with a beaming smile and invited him in. After pouring Sihanouk a glass of whisky, Pot announced that his revolution had suffered a 'minor setback' which entailed his forces making a brief, temporary excursion to the Thai border. Their Vietnamese 'brothers' would be looking after Cambodia for a while, and Sihanouk·would be in their care. They ate a vast banquet as rocket fire exploded overhead and the shouts of combatants engaged in hand-to-hand combat reached them over the evening air; Sihanouk commented afterwards that Pot had been 'the perfect host' at the sumptuous dinner, and that 'Pol Pot is mad and brutal, but in the end he does not hate me enough to kill me. He is very charming.' Pot then quickly assembled the remains of his shattered forces under the cover of darkness, and – accompanied by his acolytes, in a vast motorcade of limousines and weaponry – roared northwards out of Phnom Penh for the last time.

The Vietnamese arrived in the city at dawn on the following morning to find it totally empty. Although they had heard rumours that Pot had evacuated some of Phnom Penh's inhabitants, they were astounded to find that the entire population had vanished; all that remained, littered along the dusty boulevards, were the now-skeletal carcasses of the citizens who had been abruptly shot by Pot's revolutionary young cadres on 17 April 1975. The Vietnamese were equally astonished to discover the vast swathes of blindfolded skulls and unearthed bodies stretching over the death-zone of Choeung Ek on the city's

Dead Khmer Rouge soldiers

periphery, interspersed with the decorative cranial pyramids constructed by the Khmer Rouge cadres; when they shot their way into the blood-sodden corridors of Tuol Sleng, the final, already near-incinerated criminals of Pot's regime were still being interrogated and 'smashed' on their 'beds of death', and the Vietnamese troops had to wrench the torture instruments out of the hands of the devoted interrogators, who were still berating the terminally-tortured prisoners about their status as 'microbes' to the very end. Meanwhile, Pot and his surviving Khmer Rouge followers (many of them wounded after the battles of the preceding days) had halted their retreat at Angkor Wat, where they spent several days resting, before heading further north, to regroup in the area of Anlung Veng, in an isolated, mountainous reach of the malarial jungle alongside the Thai border. Throughout the retreat, Pot remained upbeat. He had accomplished the first stage of his great vision, and his vital work was still to come.

THE FALL OF POL POT: THE NOSTALGIA FOR ATROCITY

Pot was happy to be back in hiding in his new home on the Thai frontier, where his few thousand surviving Khmer Rouge cadres quickly subjugated the few inhabitants of the region and established a large no-go territory containing a series of compounds designed for Pot to arbitrarily move between whenever he felt threatened. Apart from his years of revolutionary glory in Phnom Penh, Pot had been living the life of a guerrilla fighter in inaccessible frontier terrains since 1962, when he had fled from the brutal police of the regal fop Sihanouk, and his short-lived Phnom Penh regime constituted more of an aberration in that insurrectionary existence rather than the summit of his revolutionary work. In fact, the habits of relentless hiding and courageous self-denial suited the diffident, retiring Pot far more than wearing silver silk suits and having shoddy concrete busts made of his suave facial features. All that was missing in his new nomadic home on the Thai frontier was the ready accessibility of opportunities to conduct merciless acts of genocide, but Pot knew that his murderous regime had been unique (even the most adroit tyrant would find it hard to thoroughly annihilate his own people to the point of near-extinction more than once), and that it had flared as an incandescent beacon of revolutionary inspiration to the oppressed peoples of the megacolonialist-dominated world, before its extinguishment by the reactionary Vietnamese hordes. In addition, the region around Anlung Veng had the advantage that it was the most gem-rich area of Cambodia, particularly in sapphires and rubies, and Pot's Khmer Rouge cadres had soon seized and begun to exploit the entirety of the gem production, quickly generating immense wealth which provided for vast weaponry and the building of compounds, and also allowed Pot to give large pay-offs to the regional Thai government on the other side of the frontier, which then agreed to leave the Khmer Rouge guerrillas alone and allowed them to extend their complex of compounds over the Thai border. This strategy of pay-offs to the corrupt Thai bureaucrats contravened Pot's detestation of money (which he had rigorously outlawed in his revolutionary eden), and the compromise tormented him. To Pot's increasing dismay, the Khmer Rouge rapidly acquired more and more wealth, and by 1981 had become a major business player in South-East Asian share-trading (where they were known informally as 'Genocide Inc.'), with a sizeable portfolio of investments in real estate and in jungle deforestation for timber production. Soon, Pot was appalled to see his sixteen-year-old revolutionary cadres swapping their mud-encrusted combat fatigues for pristine business suits and heading off for 'brainstorming' sessions with corporate partners in Bangkok and Tokyo.

Even worse, Pot was now an unwilling ally of the USA, which had decided that Pot's exiled guerrilla army constituted a far preferable alternative to the invasion force of the Communist Vietnamese, who had inflicted a devastating military defeat on the humiliated USA in 1975. The USA forced the United Nations to appoint the Khmer Rouge guerrillas as the 'authentic' government of Cambodia, while the leaders of the new colonial regime in Phnom Penh were treated as pariahs. Money and consumer products lavishly rolled in to Pot's compounds from the USA, as well as from China, which also opposed the Vietnamese Communists because of their alliance with China's great rival, the Soviet Union. Although Pot kept up with his vitriol-laden attacks on his 'megacolonialist' enemies, accusing them of being 'land swallowers and human rights violators', he now found that he was receiving the active support of almost all of the major powers, including Britain and France, against which he had railed during his years of supreme power. This support meant that Pot's great atrocities – and the permanent decimation they had inflicted on Cambodia itself – were soon transformed into a short-lived media furore that, having turned those acts into a television spectacle, then annulled them and cast them into oblivion. After Pot had been repeatedly dubbed both a 'genocidal fascist' and a 'genocidal communist' by the media, to the saturation point where the accusations against him meant nothing at all, he was quickly assimilated in the early 1980s into the global political family. The US President Ronald Reagan called Pot's massacres 'a minor hiccup', while British Prime Minister Margaret Thatcher praised Pot's sterling performance as a leader. Pot himself became a comprehensive consumer of the media, reading everything written about him. However, the worldwide media frenzy around Pot's Khmer Rouge was very quickly over, and the relieved Pot was finally left alone to get on with plotting the next stage of his great work of revolutionary slaughter.

Meanwhile, back in Phnom Penh, the Vietnamese Communists would remain in power for fourteen years, spending their time attempting to indoctrinate the terminally-disabused inhabitants of their new colony into their own revolutionary designs (which, compared to those of Pot, were anodyne in the extreme, consisting mainly of instituting peaceful agricultural collectives and opposing the USA). Since the newly-colonized population of the Pot-decimated Cambodia now consisted largely of dull-witted, in-bred peasants, and very few surviving urbanites, the nuances of the Vietnamese Communists' plans passed them by completely. The Vietnamese also attempted to revile the name of Pot, whose forces still posed a glowering military threat on their colony's northern border; they opened up Pot's now-empty Tuol Sleng Death Facility S-21 as 'Genocide Museum Number 7' and passed a law stating that, whenever anyone mentioned Pot's name, they had to add the prefix 'the contemptible' before naming Pot. Other than these innovations, the 1980s passed in a stupor of tedium for most Cambodians – after the intensive revolutionary stimulation of Pot's murderous years in power, the Vietnamese colonials presented nothing that could seize the Cambodians' attention in the way that Pot's vast carnage had. Then, on 25 September 1989, as the Communist regimes began to crumble worldwide, the colonial Vietnamese Communists abruptly abandoned Cambodia overnight, vanishing as suddenly as they had appeared and leaving the country in the hands of Sihanouk, who had been patiently biding his time in his palace. The regal fop reinstated his profligate rule exactly at the point where it had been interrupted by Pot in 1975 (often adroitly using his old strategy of presenting himself as being at loggerheads with the politicians he installed, in order to distract the attention of the Cambodians away from his monumental shopping sprees and lavish nightly banquets). Sihanouk also rigorously milked and scammed the ineffectual United Nations peace-keeping forces which occupied the devastated Cambodia in the early 1990s, and ordered the building of extravagant monuments in Phnom Penh, as symbols of his benevolent power (though these garish constructions were often left abandoned in a half-finished state, as Sihanouk lost interest and diverted the funds into new shopping projects). Sihanouk regularly appeared on Cambodia's new television channel to give maudlin addresses to his people on how he had 'sacrificed everything' for them. Soon, he had successfully reinstated the fertile and gem-rich Cambodia in its ranking as the poorest country in the world.

On the Thai frontier, Pot worked hard to re-establish the atmosphere of uncompromised carnage which his compound of the early 1970s had possessed, with its cannibalistic bodyguards and its routines of arbitrary decapitation. Pot named his main compound 'Office 87', and his new generation of sixteen-year-old revolutionary cadres revered him as 'Grandfather 87', whose beaming smile never left his attractive face as he instructed them in the necessity of relentlessly 'smashing' enemies (Pot now delivered his diatribes as a model of concision, in under six hours). Many of Pot's most committed young cadres were recruited from the rural population of the region, which had not experienced the full, unadulterated impact of Pot's great vision for a sexually-collectivized peasantry free from the malevolent illusions of family-life; as a result, Pot was eager to begin a new experiment in instituting a 'ground-zero' sexual regime within his network of compounds. Pot's four principal allies in the Khmer Rouge leadership – Ta Mok, Son Sen, Ieng Sary and Nuon Chea – had all escaped Phnom Penh in the terminal motorcade of the 'Great Apparatus', to whom they still pledged their servile, undying obeisance. But Pot's experience, in the final days of his regime, with the obsequious journalist Malcolm Caldwell had reignited his deep-rooted sense of suspicion of his sycophantic acolytes, which proved to be largely justified. Often, in the evenings, Pot would walk to a hill on the edge of his compound, in the company of two or three of his purest revolutionary cadres, and – while drinking his favourite 'Suntory' whisky – would nostalgically recount anecdotes about his forces' headlong rampage across Cambodia in 1975, undertaking gratuitous acts of atrocity as they went, in order to fulfil their mission of exterminating all of the country's traitors and of assisting the expelled inhabitants of Phnom Penh by permanently relieving them of the demands of urban life.

As Pot's years of exile on the Thai frontier went by, he intensively plotted the resurgence of Khmer Rouge domination over Cambodia. But this time, he was planning an annihilatory 'pure product' that would explode in a chain-reaction of extermination right across South-East Asia, before consuming his worldwide 'megacolonialist' enemies too, in a ferocious conflagration of arterial blood, severed body parts and tidal waves of semen. This time, he would not make the mistake of limiting his great project to Cambodia itself, which had led to accusations that he had acted out of nationalistic or racialist intentions. Certainly, Pot despised the Vietnamese, and watched with satisfaction as they vacated their colony in 1989 (although he was nonplussed to see his old enemy Sihanouk – whose unknown moment of death Pot had held in his hands for so long that it had finally been squandered – reassert his profligate grip on Cambodia). But the Vietnamese alone were not Pot's primary target for remorseless butchery. Although he had made certain, during his years in power, that all Cambodians of Vietnamese origins were meticulously included in his vast slaughter, Pot's great project was far too all-engulfing in scope to be reduced to nationalistic ambition: it was aimed at the radical transformation – through sheer atrocity – of the human anatomy itself, together with the wholesale obliteration of urban life and the final uprooting, via the capricious wielding of coruscating totalitarian power, of all human life.

Pot decided that he should commit some of his revolutionary insights to paper, despite his profound reservations about writing and visual images which had led him to outlaw all books and other media under his regime (apart from the meticulous written and photographic records of torturings and 'smashings' that had been catalogued at Tuol Sleng). Pot could not face the act of writing himself, but – during his evenings of relaxation, whisky glass in hand – he would dictate some of his revelations to the most trusted of his sixteen-year-old revolutionary cadres. The resulting nine notebooks were mistakenly believed to have been lost in the chaotic years following Pot's demise, when his most devoted cadres had been relentlessly chased through the malarial jungles by Sihanouk's brutal forces. In his self-critical, rambling dictation, Pot admitted that some of his strategies had backfired: 'We were a little excessive in our rate of extermination of megacolonialist traitors and Vietnamese agents, and exhausted our stock of contemptible conspirators too rapidly, leaving us with no fuel for our revolutionary fire... However, despite our best efforts, we did not extirpate enough microbes, and there must have been spies in our ranks who opened our borders to our contemptible brothers from Vietnam... If only we had had more human fertilizer.... If only we had had more fuel for the hot method so that our enemies could have been smashed more totally... If only we had had more of everything... Now I am tired, but I will go on...'.

In the mid-1990s, Pot's armoured compound began to disintegrate. Although the Khmer Rouge now possessed a vast arsenal of sophisticated weaponry, most of it supplied by the USA and China, it was left unused. Those of Pot's die-hard followers from the 1970s who had survived were far more attuned to wielding machetes and assorted blunt instruments, and left the mountains of digitally-operated weaponry in their packing cases. And many of Pot's new generation of followers had decided that all weaponry was obsolete, and that they would be better employed inflicting new strategies of economic global terrorism on their megacolonialist enemies, by sabotaging financial markets and precipitating all-out digital crashes. The atmosphere of Pot's compound had irreparably shifted, and the sheer revolutionary ferocity that, twenty years previously, had built Pot's extreme eden was now rapidly leaking away. Even the white-haired, seventy-year-old Pot himself – weak from malarial fever and the continuing intestinal eruptions that had assailed him since his insect-rich jungle diet of the 1960s – was now no longer demonstrating the radical zeal which had led him to envisage all sex as a compulsorily collectivized, 'ground-zero' state of anti-familial revolutionary action. He secretly married one of his cadres of peasant origin, Mea Son, and they soon had a daughter, named Sith, whom Pot would carry around on his shoulders as he volubly indoctrinated his now-disinterested cadres in their revolutionary duties against 'microbes'.

It was only in the middle of 1997, when he had less than a year left to live, that Pot realised he had allowed his revolutionary momentum to slide away. He suddenly developed a new resolve to finally carry through his great project for world-wide totalitarian and corporeal revolution, announcing in one of his last radio broadcasts: 'We will fight to the end of the world... I am going back to seek the old road.' However, Pot now had no resources left with which to carry through his determination. And this proved to be the moment when the clique of Pot's four leading acolytes broke apart, thereby validating his long-standing suspicions. Ieng Sary fled Pot's compound, allying himself with Sihanouk and his Prime Minister, Hun Sen, who had once been a Khmer Rouge cadre himself. After his forty years of utter subjugation to Pot, Ieng Sary's defection threw Pot into a state of wrath, and he sent an execution squad of his followers to 'smash' the traitor; but they too repudiated Pot and joined forces with Sihanouk. Pot also had problems with Ta Mok, who had decided that the point had come for him to oust Pot and take control of the Khmer Rouge himself; he was nostalgic for the arbitrary murderings of the Khmer Rouge's vintage years, and the two decades of stasis he had endured on the Thai frontier had driven him into a psychotic state of boredom. He planned to demote Pot to the status of 'Brother Number 6,741' and to seize the coveted Number One ranking himself, before ordering murderous incursions against Sihanouk's forces. Although Nuon Chea remained loyal to Pot, the fourth of his acolytes, Son Sen (who had been primarily responsible for overseeing the operations at Tuol Sleng), had decided to defect to the Vietnamese; this was the final straw for the ever-tolerant Pot, and at midnight on 9 June 1997, surrounded by a group of his most uncompromised revolutionary cadres, Pot burst into Son Sen's house in the compound and ferociously beat the screaming traitor to death with a lead club, leaving behind on the floor a congealed purple pulp of decimated tissue and cracked bones. Pot emerged stony-faced from the hut, drenched in smoking blood and still carrying the club, in front of the massed ranks of his followers, who had been alerted by the screams. It was the first killing which Pot had ever conducted personally, and the first time he had ever been seen without his familiar beaming smile. Pot's cadres then massacred Son Sen's entire family, and locked up Ta Mok and other potential traitors in a hut next to the compound's sewage trench.

The 'smashing' of Son Sen and his family deeply unsettled many of the younger Khmer Rouge, especially those who had never before seen an act of gratuitous extermination – the Khmer Rouge had mostly refrained from massacring the inhabitants of the region around their compound, and the vintage slaughters perpetrated by the Khmer Rouge in the 1970s had taken place before the current generation of revolutionary cadres had even been born. After a few days of uneasy muttering, almost all of the Khmer Rouge cadres decided that the time had come to usurp the archaic Pot, and on 13 June they released Ta Mok and the other traitors from their hut. Hearing that he had been betrayed by his own forces, Pot had to flee headlong from his compound, accompanied only by a small group of his most die-hard followers, who carried the now-exhausted Pot (weak from his exertions in having thoroughly culled Son Sen) through the jungle in an old hammock. Ta Mok ordered that Pot should be tracked down, and on 16 June, the Khmer Rouge caught up with Pot; his followers were either captured or escaped into the jungle. Pot was brought back to the compound and placed under house-arrest in a small wooden house at the compound's edge. In the following month, he was 'purged' from the Khmer Rouge leadership and subjected to an open-air show trial in the compound, where he sat in defiant silence as his former acolytes chanted: 'Defeat for the corrupt fascist Pot! Defeat! Defeat! Defeat for the barbarous Pot and his blood-soaked hands! Defeat! Defeat!'. Pot was sentenced to be detained at the caprice of Ta Mok and his equally-brutish associates for the rest of his life. The event was recorded and transmitted by a specially-invited Japanese television crew.

Although Pot remained completely silent at his trial, and refused to speak openly to the television journalists whom Ta Mok (who now viewed the ailing Pot as his personal property) brought to the compound, he made his final pronouncements on the blighted twentieth century to his surviving followers, telling them that only he and his idol Stalin had possessed any revolutionary vision capable of shattering the stupor into which human beings had fallen, which had rendered them vulnerable to the supreme indignities of colonial power and other forms of oppression – but revolutionary will itself was lethal, and caused the most dangerous but necessary experiments in history. However, few of the Khmer Rouge cadres were listening to Pot's diatribes any longer. He became an almost-forgotten figure in the compound as Ta Mok attempted to discipline the vacillating cadres and prepare them for brutal assaults on Sihanouk's forces. Pot's teenaged guards installed a blaring television set in his room and spent their time yelling at one another and watching the first series of *Buffy The Vampire Slayer*. When Pot chastised the slouching ex-cadres on the deterioration of their revolutionary determination, his captors eyed him with contempt. The power of Pot was finished. He was allowed to remain with his wife, who treated him for malarial fevers.

After his capture, Pot's new owners allowed him to become the leased property of a Thai prostitution circle, which specialized in acquiring 'prestigious' celebrities for their clients to engage in anal intercourse with. All those who passed through Bangkok's extreme sex scene in the first months of 1998 heard about the 'special deal' being offered by the Black Hand Sex Agency, which (in exchange for $3,750 in cash) involved a luxury tour eastwards to the Cambodian frontier for a short 'quality encounter' with the 'contemptible tyrant Pol Pot', with two or three deflowerings of seven-year-old virgins (of either sex) thrown in, en route to the frontier, as added promotional attractions. The Black Hand Agency announced to a selection of wealthy stockbroking companies and underworld gangs in Tokyo and Shanghai that it had 'privatized' Pol Pot as an exclusive commodity, and that their 'product' was available to entertain only the most distinguished corporate clients. Those who saw the television images of Pot on his deathbed were often baffled as to why he now had dyed jet-black hair (styled like that of Elvis Presley), when it was known that for many years his hair had been snow-white; the explanation was that he was always 'cosmetically enhanced' in expectation of his nightly clients. A garish hut was set up at the perimeter of the Khmer Rouge compound with several rooms lavishly decorated according to the diverse styles of a Japanese 'love-hotel', each with pornographic television channels transmitted from seven-foot-square digital screens. Pot suffered his sexual humiliation stoically, commenting only that a professional revolutionary's life was a difficult one and often full of trials. But, as the weeks of relentless buggery went by, he began to confide that he had grown accustomed to his new life of abject sexual slavery, and even preferred it to his former metier of genocidal dictator and revolutionary mass-murderer.

Pot grew weaker from the combined effects of his malarial fevers, his long-standing intestinal problems (which occasionally resulted in his liberally-spattered clients having to be given full refunds), and the terminal ferocity with which he had 'smashed' Son Sen. And, as it became clear that he was being buggered into annihilation, his clients had to be reduced in number, although after one of his final sessions – involving a number of sturdy Thai businessmen – Pot reported that he had experienced a revelatory 'anal holocaust' which had served to give him the inspiration for an entirely new revolutionary project. However, by the beginning of March 1998, it was clear that Pot's great vision would never be carried through. His health was now rapidly deteriorating, exacerbated by exhaustion, and Ta Mok needed to work fast to get the maximum amount of potential exploitation out of his genocidal product. At the same time, Sihanouk's forces were starting to close in on the compound, urgently incited by the treacherous Ieng Sary to capture Pot and put him on public trial in front of the world's news media ahead of his imminent demise. Once the ailing Pot had expired and departed for the Shining Land, both his commercial and atrocity-criminal values would revert to zero just as surely as his murderous revolution had returned Cambodia itself to zero on 17 April 1975.

The embattled Khmer Rouge, under Ta Mok's inept leadership, had to abandon their compound at the end of March after Sihanouk's forces had attempted to encircle it. Sihanouk himself had no desire to see Pot put on trial, since he remembered with gratitude that the ever-charming Pot had capriciously spared his life nineteen years earlier, on the night of the wayward totalitarian's abrupt exit from Phnom Penh, and had given the regal fop a splendid banquet to boot. As a result, Sihanouk's forces held back from the temporary camp established by Ta Mok during Pot's last days. Pot himself, his newly jet-black dyed hair contrasting with his pallid skin, was occasionally moved to secret locations for his assignations in a large white Toyota van with mud-caked windows. Otherwise, he rested on his plywood bed in a small shack within Ta Mok's camp. Finally, on the evening of 15 April 1998, Pot – the great bringer of death – himself died. He had been listening to the Voice of America radio station, on which news reports about his own ostensibly-imminent public trial were being transmitted. Pot was unconcerned: if necessary, he would protect himself, as ever, with self-effacement and a black silence. Pot's wife, preparing food in the adjoining room, suddenly heard a slight gasp of breath, and found Pot had died quietly. Blood was leaking out of his nose, and she packed his nostrils with cotton wool. The Khmer Rouge cadres arrived and coldly viewed the carcass of the 'Great Apparatus'.

Pot's funeral had to be conducted almost immediately, since his body was soon putrefying in the humid, mosquito-ridden air of the frontier zone where the temporary camp was situated. In a jungle clearing, Pot's body was placed naked, together with his Book of Death, in a large packing case that had been used for the delivery of US weapons to the Khmer Rouge, and covered with a few tattered black rags of clothing and the broken wreckage of his plywood bed (his only other possessions). Then the debris was soaked in petrol and set light to, burning up with a roar. Every last trace of Pot was consumed in the haphazard cremation, idly watched by six or seven of the Khmer Rouge cadres. Before long, Sihanouk's forces would close in on the makeshift camp, and many of the terrified Khmer Rouge had already abandoned Ta Mok and slipped away into the jungle. Ta Mok, desperate to squeeze the very last shreds of media exposure from Pot, gave an interview in front of the funeral pyre to the Japanese NHK television channel, and commented (evidently furious that his livelihood had been snatched away from him): 'Pol Pot has died, like an over-ripe papaya.

Nobody killed him, nobody poisoned him – he was tired... Now it's all over – he's finished. He has no more power, he is no more than cow shit. Cow shit is more important than him. We are going to mix Pol Pot's ashes with cow shit and use him for fertilizer.' Pot's cremation-site was officially nominated a Cambodian 'tourist attraction' in 2002.

Among the twentieth century's great projects of annihilation, Pol Pot's totalitarian vision of slaughter and corporeal upheaval for Cambodia matched and even superseded that of Stalin, both in its crazed lucidity and in the sheer determination with which Pot and his followers carried it through, engendering millions of tortured and brutalized casualties. Like Stalin, Pot was reviled at his death and nonchalantly consigned to oblivion, only to subsequently burst back into prominence as a prescient and revealing figure for the new century, both for East Asia and the entire world. In Cambodia itself, the residue of the Khmer Rouge was gradually absorbed into power by Sihanouk's government; only the brutal Ta Mok and the midget-commandant of Tuol Sleng, the born-again Christian Kaing Kek Ieu, were ever imprisoned for their participation in Pot's revolutionary work. The country continued to endure a regime of saturation-level corruption, only exacerbated by the presence of the inept United Nations forces which were dispatched to the devastated country in the 1990s. In the years after his demise, the Cambodian peasantry began to grow nostalgic for the regime of Pot, who – as he himself had intended – came to be ranked alongside the twelfth-century Angkor leper-Emperor Jayavarman VII for their supremely despotic reigns of autocratic and sexual cruelty. While Jayavarman VII left behind the vast splendour of the Angkor Wat temple-city (which Pot had planned to destroy, though in the end it became his refuge), Pot handed down a less tangible legacy: a lethal, permanent scar of negation on the face of the human species itself. Pot's theory and practice of genocide – devised during long years in his isolated jungle compounds and then inflicted upon Cambodia during a short-lived period of power – proved to be uniquely resilient, even within a mediatized world in which the twentieth century's holocausts, genocides and atrocities are incessantly eroded and diluted to the point of

interchangeability. Pot's zones of slaughter – etched out around his depopulated cities in swathes of skulls – provide a salutary marker for the future of urban life and political power. Pot's acts remain a jet of white-hot flame directed straight at the eye of humanity.

Index

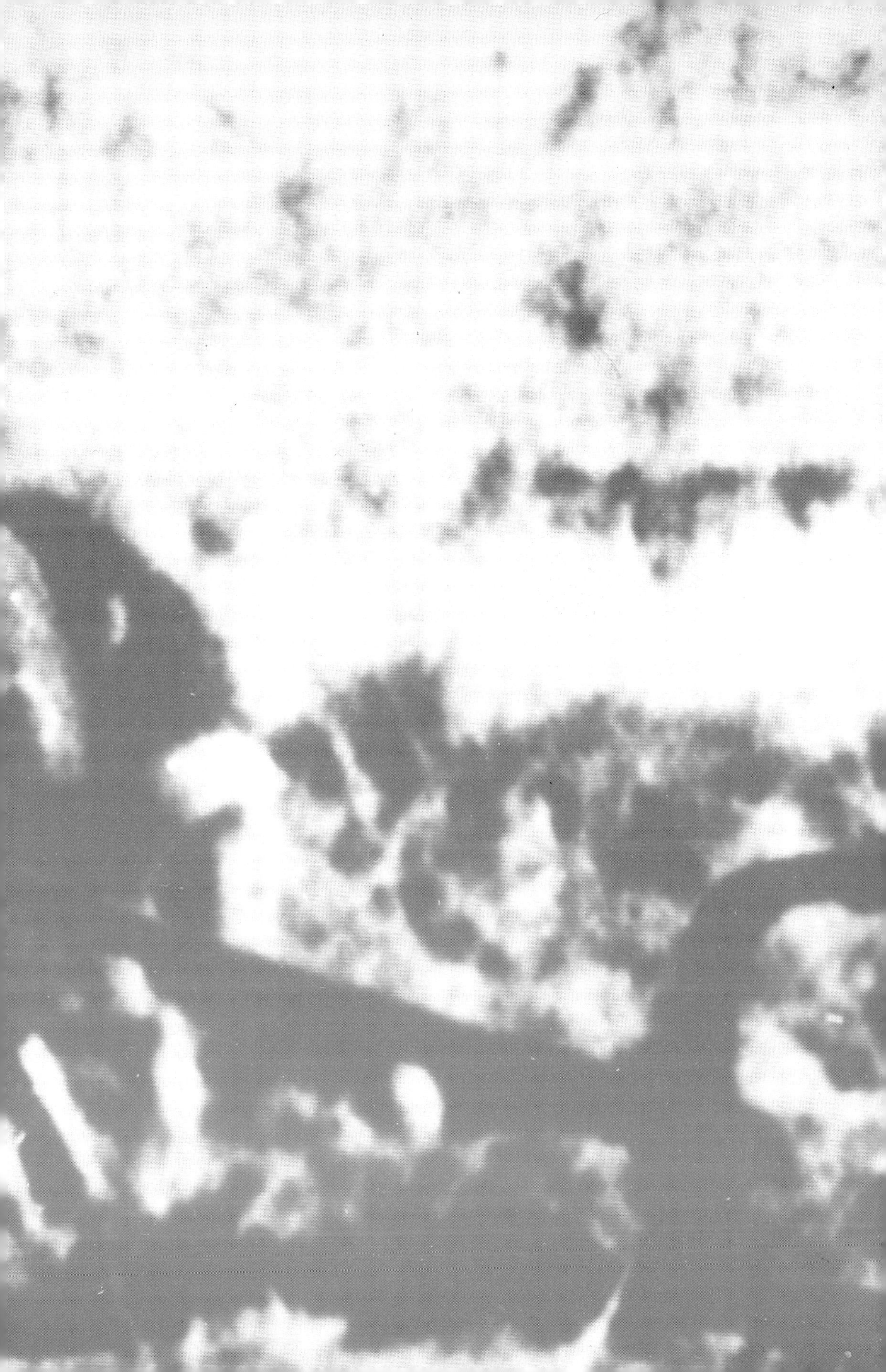

www.creationbooks.com